Additional Praise for
Retire Secure! For Same-Sex Couples

"Jim has generously pledged the proceeds from this book to Freedom to Marry and naturally, I appreciate that. But what I really appreciate is his bringing his expertise to bear on helping the couples for whom we have already won the freedom to marry."

> —Evan Wolfson (from the foreword)
> Founder and President, Freedom to Marry
> A national campaign dedicated to marriage equality for same-sex couples

"Now that marriage equality is a reality, we have a lot of brushing up to do. Estate planning, tax laws, medical benefits, housing rights, healthcare and on and on. They have granted us the right to marry. The responsibility of understanding the law is ours. Here's your guide."

> —Harvey Fierstein, Tony Award Winning Actor & Playwright

"The DOMA decision advanced social opportunities for legally-married same-sex couples. But DOMA was also a game changer for tax planning, if you know what changed and what to do about it. Lucky for you, IRA and tax planning expert, Jim Lange has the answers in *Retire Secure! for Same-Sex Couples.* It's thorough and very well done. Jim provides a comprehensive road map to all the new retirement and estate planning strategies that were not previously available to same-sex couples. But they are now, and couples who wish to take advantage of them to enhance their options, increase their wealth, cut their taxes and live with financial security should dive into this gem. Jim Lange delves into life's most critical financial planning aspects including taxes, retirement benefits, optimizing your joint Social Security benefits, passing wealth to each other and to loved ones and even helps you with the intricacies of health insurance. This is all new and *Retire Secure! for Same-Sex Couples* is your how-to financial guide going forward. No question, this can only benefit people's lives."

> —Ed Slott, CPA
> "America's IRA Expert"

Best-selling author, James Lange, has a richly deserved reputation for providing well-considered, practical advice on investing, retirement planning and tax management. Now he has turned his attention to the tremendous opportunities that have become available since the Supreme Court struck down a key provision of the Defense of Marriage Act. Same-sex couples will do themselves a huge favor by reading this book and acting on its advice."

> —Burton G. Malkiel, Author
> 11th Edition of *A Random Walk Down Wall Street*,

"With the Supreme Court ruling in U.S. v. Windsor holding that Section 3 of the Defense of Marriage Act (DOMA) is unconstitutional, planning for same-sex couples has been radically changed. Jim Lange has written an invaluable guide for both practitioners and their clients as to how to plan in this new environment. This book is an outstanding edition for the reader. The changing world of health insurance and Social Security benefits is thoroughly discussed in the book."

—Sid Kess, CPA, J.D., LL.M., Author/Speaker
More than 1 Million CPAs have taken Kess Courses

"*Retire Secure! for Same-Sex Couples* makes it easy to learn the answers to all your questions about this topic, including many you might not have thought to ask."

—Kaye A. Thomas
Author, *Go Roth!*

"*Retire Secure!* is a must-read book for same-sex couples who want financial security for themselves and their heirs. James Lange applies his legal and tax experience with common sense, sound calculations, and action steps in an "easy-to-read format.""

—Ron Kelemen, CFP®, Author,
The Confident Retirement Journey—Your Personal & Financial Roadmap
The H Group, Inc. Salem, OR

"*Retire Secure!* is a must read for LGBT couples wondering what is the best path for them pursue in regard to marriage. For many of my friends and family who are wrestling with this important issue, they often care more about fairness and access to marriage as an institution. Jim brings to the community a clear roadmap for how they can rationally approach the critical responsibilities and opportunities that might be afforded to them financially. I applaud his effort to use his legal and accounting expertise to help the community in such a practical manner."

—Tim McCarthy, Author,
The Safe Investor: How to Make Your Money Grow in a Volatile Economy

"*Retire Secure! for Same-Sex Couples* is a must read, providing practical guidance on important planning issues. Financial planning for same-sex couples is evolving in response to changing federal and state laws, and Jim Lange's book provides invaluable advice in an easy to digest manner."

—Daniel S. Kern, President and CIO, Advisor Partners

"Like a breath of fresh air, the doors are being kicked open that address what society is demanding – and that is same-sex couples are entitled to have their concerns and issues dealt with openly, consciously and appropriately. Kudos to Jim, for writing this terrific resource for planners, same-sex couples and other professionals who will benefit greatly from the knowledge, information and clarity provided. As a Financial Life Planner, these issues are essential to good practice and knowledge to help clients lead the life that is most important to them. This book is a terrific resource and each topic is clearly explained with concise and easy to understand examples provided. Great job!"

> —Michael F. Kay, CFP®, President, Financial Life Focus, LLC

"*Retire Secure!* provides a wealth of valuable information. It covers retirement plans, Social Security, income taxes, trusts and estate and inheritance tax issues. Given the recent Supreme Court decision and changes in the tax code, this book is a must read for same-sex couples."

> —Mel Lindauer, Forbes.com, ColumnistCo-Author,
> *The Bogleheads' Guide to Investing*
> *The Bogleheads' Guide to Retirement Planning*

"In *Retire Secure! For Same-Sex Couples*, Lange not only jigsaws the pieces together for the LGBT community, but also provides great advice for the straight community. By using well thought out examples and clear graphs, even the most finance-challenged among us can follow along and be better able to meet our retirement goals."

> —Bart Astor, Author, *Roadmap for the Rest of Your Life*

"The IRS, Social Security and many other government agencies have rules that are different for straight and gay couples. Jim Lange, a retirement expert, has written *Retire Secure! for Same-Sex Couples* to increase their wealth, cut their taxes, and dramatically increase their financial security. This is a book I can highly recommend for the gay community and those who work to serve them. All proceeds will go to the civil rights organization, Freedom to Marry."

> —Taylor Larimore, Co-Author, *The Bogleheads' Guide to Investing*
> *The Bogleheads' Guide to Retirement Planning*

"Jim Lange's book fills a much needed void by providing sound financial advice to same-sex couples. Implementing his recommendations can reduce taxes and permit same-sex couples to retire with dignity."

> —Dan Solin, Author of the *Smartest* series of books

"An eye-opening book! Read it now and secure your future. Delay and you'll pay later. I urge you to read this book right now."

—Dr. Joe Vitale, Author, *Attract Money Now*

"Jim did a great job (again!) at reducing complex planning concepts to understandable action steps. The planning landscape for same-sex couples has and continues to change radically. You need accurate and current guidance. Harnessing the power of compounding investment earnings, and Jim's sage advice, will give you the best odds of a secure financial future."

—Martin M. Shenkman, CPA, MBA, JD
Author of 36 books and 700+ articles

"Recent changes in state and federal laws mean that same-sex couples can now claim many of the spousal benefits associated with IRAs, 401(k)s, estate taxes, Social Security, and government-subsidized health insurance. *Retire Secure! for Same-Sex Couples* helps you navigate the bewildering maze of rules and regulations, and avoid tax-planning mistakes that could sabotage your retirement plans. Jim Lange explains how you and your partner can manage two incomes, save on health insurance, maximize Social Security benefits for both of you, and transfer your wealth to your heirs. It is never too early (or too late!) to start planning."

—Martha Maeda, Author
Retire Rich With Your Roth IRA, Roth 401k and Roth 403b: Investment Strategies for Your Roth IRA Explained Simply

"Jim Lange has taken the question-marks out of planning for same-sex couples. I highly recommend you not only read, but use this book!"

—Deena B Katz, CFP®
Associate Professor, Texas Tech University
Department of Personal Financial Planning

"In *Retire Secure! For Same Sex Couples*, attorney and IRA expert Jim Lange explains how marriage can enhance the value of IRAs and Social Security, and how same-sex couples can now take advantage of these benefits.

—Bruce Steiner, Attorney
Kleinberg, Kaplan, Wolff & Cohen, P.C.

"Jim provides some invaluable strategies for many loving couples who are currently deprived of the same rights as their fellow citizens. His suggestions could mean thousands of dollars to couples who happen to live in certain states. Change is the only changeless norm when it comes to retirement planning."

—Dan Keppel, Author,
Maximize Your Social Security Benefits and Retirement Income

"*Retire Secure! For Same-Sex Couples* shows you great ideas to help you achieve the most important financial goal of your life. Make your money last and go further than you ever thought possible."

—Brian Tracy, Speaker, Sales Trainer, Author, *Getting Rich Your Own Way*

"There are so many laws both federal and state and they affect same-sex couples differently. As a CPA and an attorney, James Lange has more than 30 years in estate- and retirement-planning experience. He has made a specialty of retirement planning for same-sex couples."

—Dan Poynter, Author, Publisher and Speaker

"It's about time! CPA and attorney Jim Lange has written the essential financial guide for same-sex couples. Brimming with examples, case studies, and easily understood graphs, Lange has laid out a path that is simple to understand, simple to follow, and extremely valuable. If you're part of the LGBT community, you need this book!"

—Jan Cullinane, Author, *The Single Woman's Guide to Retirement*

"Jim Lange has written a wonderful book for all committed couples – same-sex or opposite sex – who are considering marriage. Once you reach retirement age, marriage becomes the best way of preserving income and wealth for the partner who survives.'

—Jane Bryant Quinn, Columnist, *AARP* and Editorial Director, *Daily Voice,*
Author, *Making the Most of Your Money NOW, A Complete Guide to Personal Finance*

RETIRE SECURE!

FOR SAME-SEX COUPLES

James Lange, CPA/Attorney

Lange Legal Group, LLC

2200 Murray Avenue

Pittsburgh, PA 15217

412-521-2732

admin@paytaxeslater.com

Copyright 2014

Table of Contents

Foreword by Evan Wolfson 1

An Update For Our Pennsylvania Readers 3

Acknowledgments 7

Introduction (Please Don't Skip) 13

The Essence of the Book Boiled Down to 9 Graphs 21

**1. The Defense of Marriage Act (DOMA) and the
   Consequences of the Windsor Decision** 31

    Chapter One Overview 31

    United States v. Windsor: 32

        The Back-Story 32

        *The Supreme Court Ruled DOMA Unconstitutional Because
   of Unequal Treatment in the Federal Estate Tax* 34

        *Internal Revenue Service Extends the Windsor Decision in
   Revenue Ruling 2013-17* 34

        The State of Celebration vs. the State of Domicile 36

    My "Eureka!" Moment 36

    Pennsylvania and Other States That Don't Recognize Same-Sex
   Marriage 40

    Tying the Knot or Not: Financial Considerations for Same-Sex
   Couples 42

    As the Legal Landscape Changes, What Should You Do? 44

2. Optimizing IRAs & Retirement Plans for Same-Sex Couples 53

Overview of IRAs and Retirement Plans 53

Background: The Power of Retirement Plans While Working 54

Background: Which Dollars Should You Spend First in Retirement? 58

The Impact of Marriage on the Accumulation Years 61

How Should You Plan for Your IRA and Retirement Plan After Your Death? 65

The Tax Law for IRAs and Retirement Accounts as It Relates to Same-Sex Couples 66

Down to the Nitty Gritty 69

Who Can Inherit an IRA? 69

A Case Study of a Same-Sex Couple, Reviewing Finances for Surviving Spouse if One Person Dies and Leaves His IRA to His Partner/Spouse 73

The Couple Remains Unmarried (Given Current Laws on Inherited IRAs) 75

The Couple Marries 76

More Bad News if the Couple Remains Unmarried (Under Proposed Laws for Inherited IRAs) 81

Let's Review the Numbers 82

The Case Study Continues for the Second Generation of Heirs, Reviewing Finances for the Child of the Surviving Partner 83
The Couple Remains Unmarried (Given Current Laws on Inherited IRAs) 81

The Couple Remains Unmarried (Given Current Laws on Inherited IRAs).. 84

The Couple Marries 86

Further Complications for the Child if the Couple Remains Unmarried and the "Stretch" Laws Change 87

Let's Summarize the Numbers for the Case Study 90

First Let's Simply Look at the Finances for the Couple 90

Managing an IRA After Death Is Very Important for The Well-Being of The Next Generation 91

Proposed Regulation Changes 94

3. Same-Sex Couples and Social Security Benefits 98

Significant Social Security Benefits for Married Couples 98

The Big Picture 100

Chapter Overview on Social Security 104

My Big Assumption… but I Could be Wrong 105

The Basics 107

Comparison of Taking Social Security at Age 62 or Age 108

Running the Numbers for a Single Social Security Recipient 110

Delay Claiming Benefits to Provide Long-Term Security for Your Surviving Spouse 114

Scenario 1: Married, Surviving Spouse Collects Survivor Benefit 114

Scenario 2: Unmarried, No Survivor Benefit for Surviving Partner 115

Coming Out Later in Life and Protecting Your Partner 117

The Current Policy of the Social Security Administration 119

Strategies to Maximize Social Security Benefits 121

Spousal Benefits 123

Using the "Apply and Suspend" Strategy to Enhance Cumulative Benefits 124

Here's How It Works 125

Should the "Apply and Suspend" Technique Factor into a Decision to Get Married? 127

An Alternative Strategy: Claim Now, Claim More Later .. 134

Summary of the Key Points and Five Strategies You Can Use To Maximize Your Social Security Benefits 135

4. Income Tax Changes for Married Same-Sex Couples 141

How the Federal Income Tax Has Changed for Married Same-Sex Couples 141

All Legally Married Same-Sex Couples Should Review Their Federal Income Tax Returns and Make the Appropriate Changes 143

Are There Good Financial Reasons to Get Legally Married? 145

The Advantages and Disadvantages of Marriage on Your Federal Income Tax Return 145

Examples of the Marriage Bonus from Filing Jointly 146

Example of the Marriage Penalty from Filing Jointly 147

Maybe Marriage is a Good Idea if You are Selling Your

House 147

Your Age Might Also Factor into Your Decision 148

Further Financial Considerations to Have on Your Radar 145

What Is Your Filing Status for State Income Tax Purposes? 150

5. Trusts for Same-Sex Couples 153

Providing For Your Partner after You Die While Still Protecting Your Beneficiaries (Who Are Not the Same People as Your Partner's Beneficiaries) 153

How a Standard Trust Works 155

How a Traditional Trust Defines Income 157

Use a Different Definition to Define Income 158

A Concept Called the Total Return Trust 159

Avoiding Conflict among Beneficiaries and Other Issues.. 160

A Simple Solution When You Want to Provide for Your Partner and Other Heirs 161

Life Insurance 162

Providing for Your Partner without Extended Family Constraints.163

An Alternative Solution is an Agreement with Your Partner 164

Trust Basics and Situations When a Trust May Be Appropriate ... 168

Naming a Trust as the Beneficiary of an IRA 169

Using a Trust to Provide Protection for a Minor 169

Trusts for Adult Beneficiaries 171

Giving Your Beneficiaries the Right to Disclaim to Other Beneficiaries 172

A Trust for a Special Needs Beneficiary 173

Choosing a Trustee for Your Trust 174

Is Using a Trust a Good Idea for You? 175

6. The Changing World of Health Insurance 177

Introduction: The Affordable Care Act 177

Filing Requirements for Tax Credits 178

New Tax Regulations for Employer Provided Health Care Plans for Same-Sex Couples 180

The Financial Implications of Marriage on Same-Sex Health Insurance Options 184

7. Federal and State Gift, Estate, and Inheritance Taxes ... 186

An Overview of Transfer Taxes 186

Gifting Between Spouses in Non-Recognition States Can Eliminate Inheritance Taxes 189

Additional Gift Considerations 190

8. Putting All the Pieces Together 193

A Case Study Spanning the Later Years of Life for a Same-Sex Couple 199

Finances for this Couple While They are Both Living—Using All of the Advice in this Book 202

Let's Take Our Case Study to the Next Phase in Life—the Death of One Spouse/Partner 207

Finances for the Surviving Partner/Spouse—Using All of the Advice in this Book 208

The Case Study Continues With the Second Death—What About the Next Generation? 220

Let's Take a Look at the Long Term Growth Potential for the Couple's Heir if They Follow All of the Advice in This Book 220

Final Note 224

Appendix: How We "Run the Numbers" 226

Foreword

We've come a long, long way in our campaign to win the freedom to marry for same-sex couples nationwide – but with all our momentum and progress, we still have lots more to do.

Forty percent of Americans now live in freedom-to-marry states (up from zero a decade ago), and there are now married same-sex couples and their families in every corner of the country, giving still more non-gay people the chance to join the majority of Americans nationwide in favor of ending marriage discrimination.

But winning is not yet won, and we are not yet done. Even as waves of marriage cases make their way through the courts, we must continue to change hearts and minds and show decision-makers – elected officials, judges, and, yes, the justices of the Supreme Court – that all of America is ready for the freedom to marry.

Thanks to our movement's 2013 win before the United States Supreme Court, striking down the heart of the federal so-called "Defense of Marriage Act," the federal government has now gone from being the Number 1 discriminator against gay couples to putting its moral, and legal, weight on the side of our families, the Constitution, and the freedom to marry. When it comes to federal programs and purposes (from birth to death, with taxes in between), the federal government now rightly respects gay married couples in every state as what they are – married – even though many states still (for now) discriminate. But that patchwork of state discrimination and disrespect continues to burden families, businesses, employers, and couples planning their lives, dealing with life's ups and downs, and pursuing happiness.

To help alleviate some of the burden, tax, retirement, and estate planning expert Jim Lange is stepping forward to add his voice. Jimmy (as I knew him in high school *um-um-um* years ago…) has written *Retire Secure for Same-Sex Couples* to help married same-sex couples navigate the complexities of retirement planning amid all this momentum, change, and patchwork legislation. It's the latest in a series of retirement-advice books he has authored, to great acclaim.

I am no tax expert, but it's clear to me that *Retire Secure for Same-Sex Couples* raises the right questions, gives lots of excellent advice, provides compelling examples, and backs up its claims with numerical analysis—*running the numbers, as Jim calls it. Retire Secure for Same-Sex Couples* is a solid, helpful, mostly easy read on the application of tax, IRA, retirement, and death issues (for any married couple, actually) that offers an easy-to-understand analysis of the differences and benefits applicable to same-sex couples.

Because the law, like our movement to finish the job, is still incomplete and evolving – and because every couple's situation is so different and some big things are still unsettled or downright unfair for all same-sex couples – the book may not (in fact cannot) produce ironclad solutions for all. But, it will challenge and help same-sex couples to think about what is right for them and point them in the right direction. While people may still need to consult their own tax and estate-planning advisers, and, in some cases, Freedom to Marry's legal partners such as Lambda Legal, Gay & Lesbian Advocates & Defenders (GLAD), National Center for Lesbian Rights (NCLR), and the ACLU, Jim's advice and recommendations are a good starting point both for couples and for legal advocates for the freedom to marry.

Jim has generously pledged the proceeds from this book to Freedom to Marry, to support the work our campaign still must do to win marriage nationwide – and naturally, I appreciate that. But what I really appreciate is his bringing his expertise to bear on helping the couples for whom we have already won the freedom to marry. They, like all married couples, want to make strong, smart decisions and want and deserve to enjoy the security and opportunities that marriage as well as good financial planning brings.

I am all about winning, and we all win when families are stronger and the law is fairer. And who – even an activist – doesn't want to retire secure?

—**Evan Wolfson**

Founder and President of Freedom to Marry, A national campaign dedicated to marriage equality for same-sex couples

An Update For Our Pennsylvania Readers

On May 20, 2014, the gay marriage ban in Pennsylvania was overturned by U.S. District Judge John E. Jones III. In addition, Pennsylvania will now recognize same-sex marriages performed in other states that recognize same-sex marriage. Governor Tom Corbett has announced that he will not appeal the decision, and for the first time in the state's history, same-sex couples are now permitted to marry. This is wonderful news for the residents of our state who have been waiting for a long time to marry their same-sex partners, but it also means that some of the information in this book as it relates to Pennsylvania residents has become outdated (as, frankly, I hoped it would become). Rather than rewrite the book, I thought it would be simpler to provide Pennsylvania residents with a summary of the areas in which their lives will be affected as a consequence of the Pennsylvania decision.

First, if you're counting, there are now 32 states that *do not* recognize same-sex marriage – the original text references 33 states. Chapter 1 states that there are 17 jurisdictions that allow same-sex couples to legally marry, but, as of May 20, 2014, that number has risen - Pennsylvania became the 18th state (plus the District of Columbia) to do so.

Next, there are several references in the book to the federal criteria of "The State of Celebration vs. the State of Domicile," as well as recommendations that readers consider marrying in a state that does recognize same-sex marriage. As of May 20, 2014, same-sex couples who reside in Pennsylvania no longer have to travel out of state to get married – unless, of course, they want to – in order to enjoy the same benefits as straight married couples. Let's examine some of those benefits in greater detail.

- *Chapters 1, 4 and 5* discuss some odd Pennsylvania conundrums that, I'm sure, legally married same-sex couples will be very happy to see go by the wayside. In 2013, legally married (in another state) same-sex couples who lived in Pennsylvania were required to file their Federal tax returns as "Married," but their State returns as "Single." Those taxpayers will finally be able to file both their 2014 Federal *and* Pennsylvania returns as "Married," and they also have the option to file amended Federal returns for up to three years prior, if it makes financial sense for them to refile as "Married." (Marital status does not affect the amount of state tax that Pennsylvania residents pay, so filing amended state returns will not be necessary.)

- ***Chapter 1*** recommends that your wills and trusts be prepared based on current laws, but include special provisions in case same-sex marriage becomes legalized in Pennsylvania. Now that the state recognizes same-sex marriage, such highly customized estate planning documents likely ***will not*** be necessary.

- The beneficiary of a deceased same-sex partner used to be subject to a 15% Pennsylvania inheritance tax whether they had been unmarried or legally married (in another state), and it was my recommendation that wealthier couples consider either making large financial gifts in order to avoid that tax, or purchase life insurance to pay the tax. Going forward, those strategies will be irrelevant because those same couples ***will not pay*** Pennsylvania inheritance taxes on their spouse's assets (the same as straight married couples).

- Finally, from the human perspective, the surviving spouse of a legally married same-sex couple now has, barring extenuating circumstances, sole authority in all matters pertaining to the disposition of their spouse's remains in Pennsylvania – prior to this ruling, a same-sex spouse couldn't even be named on a death certificate.

- ***Chapter 2*** discusses the benefits of marriage as it relates to IRA's and retirement plans. Indeed, the benefits are so significant that from the federal perspective, including both income taxes and estate taxes, I recommend that all committed same-sex couples consider the financial advantages of getting married. (Please reread that chapter if you are on the fence about it.) But now, there is no need to travel to another state to marry to receive the same favorable federal tax treatment that the survivor of a straight married couple would receive on their deceased spouse's IRA or retirement plan. Now if you marry in Pennsylvania, you will assure your surviving spouse of a much better standard of living in his or her retirement than if you had not married.

- Pennsylvania does not currently tax retirement income, so the change in the law will have no effect on your state income taxes. There will be a significant change with respect to state inheritance taxes, though - an individual who inherited a retirement plan from a legally married same-sex spouse, used to have to pay the state's highest inheritance tax rate of 15%.

- In many cases, this amounted to a significant amount of money. Now, that same individual will pay nothing in state inheritance tax.

- *Chapters 1 and 3* both show, if you are a Pennsylvania resident, the monthly benefit that you would have been eligible for from Social Security, was "in question." This was because, unlike the Internal Revenue Service, the Social Security Administration recognizes same-sex marriages *in states that recognize same-sex marriages*. If you are legally married, but do not live in a state that recognizes same-sex marriage, you are not currently eligible for spousal Social Security benefits. The Social Security Administration recognized the inconsistency in their position and encouraged same-sex couples in all states to apply, but asked you to be patient as they develop and begin to implement new policies on this subject. Well, legally married same-sex couples who live in Pennsylvania don't need to wait any longer – they can now receive Social Security benefits based on their own earnings record, or the earnings record of their spouse if it is higher. Remember, though, that the decision about when and how to apply for Social Security benefits can have a far greater impact on your financial security than what the staff at your local Social Security office might lead you to believe. Decisions about timing Social Security benefits should not be done without first talking to a trusted advisor.

- In the same context, please have a second look at the graph on page 80, which illustrates what happens if Dr. Dan had used the "Apply and Suspend" technique for his Social Security benefits, and subsequently died. This graph takes in to consideration a 15% inheritance tax assessed on Dr. Dan's retirement plan. Since Pennsylvania now recognizes same-sex marriage, this tax will no longer be assessed at his death, which would make the difference between those two scenarios even more dramatic.

You should also have a look at the graph on Page 131, which illustrates the difference between taking my advice and ignoring it. The steep decline in assets at Baker Bob's age 80 was due to the 15% Pennsylvania inheritance tax he owed on Dr. Dan's estate. Now that Pennsylvania recognizes same-sex marriage and the inheritance tax no longer applies to the surviving spouse, the argument for marriage will be even stronger.

It has been a long time coming, but I am happy to see that Pennsylvania has finally made this change to their law. Same-sex Pennsylvania couples who marry will finally be treated fairly, with the same dignity and respect as straight married couples. Since this represents new territory for you, I encourage you to talk with a trusted advisor about the specifics of your own situation, so that you fully understand how these changes will affect you and your partner or possibly your spouse.

Acknowledgments

Retire Secure! For Same-Sex Couples could not have been written without the work and dedication of many others. I am indebted to a few individuals whose contributions were invaluable.

Steven T. Kohman, Certified Public Accountant, Certified Specialist in Retirement Planning, Certified Specialist in Estate Planning, has worked for me for over 18 years, and was the senior "number cruncher" for the book. Steve combines his extensive tax background with his superb quantitative and computer skills. Steve's quantitative analysis, evidenced in the graphs and charts throughout the book, presents compelling proof of the fundamental concepts that make up the backbone of *Retire Secure! For Same-Sex Couples*.

Shirl Trefelner, CPA, also made major contributions to the "number crunching" effort in the book and proved amazingly adept at taking Steve's initial analysis and further refining it with even more scenarios. She was particularly sensitive to many of the nuances in the graphs and analysis. She was particularly generous with her time, and she didn't complain about doing the work despite a heavy tax season workload.

Matt Schwartz, Esq., is an exceptionally bright and gifted IRA and estate attorney who has worked with me for 11 years. I am proud to have him as a colleague. He works closely with my clients and me to complete the documentation necessary to implement our recommended planning solutions.

Vickie Walker, JD, did much of the legal research and some of the early drafting for *Retire Secure! For Same-Sex Couples*. Her enthusiasm for same-sex couples to cut taxes and increase financial security is infectious.

Karen Mathias, Esq., is our resident Social Security expert and nit-picked us to death to get the Social Security chapter exactly correct (or at least tried to) with the legally correct language. I kept trying to keep it simple. She wanted it technically perfect. Ultimately, we compromised; the chapter, somewhat, though not completely, satisfied my desire for simplicity, and somewhat, though not completely, satisfied her desire for being technically perfect.

Cynthia Nelson, our editor plus, has been working with me for over 15 years. During this period, she has had full editing and writing responsibilities for virtually all my published works. She is a rare find. She cuts through some of the technical and legal jargon that I sometimes fall into and expresses complex thoughts in a way the lay reader can understand. She also allows me to express my humanity, and she adds touches of her own that make reading the book a better experience.

Eric Emerson, our internet marketing director, took it upon himself to put our ragged Word document into an "In Design" format and made the book look great.

Carol Palmer is another one of my employees who helped with editing and exuded an enthusiasm that was infectious.

Thanks to Dave McCoy for your great cartoons. I had to look up his name because I think of him as Dave Toons.

To John Kremer, my "rock-star book consultant," thank you for your patience with a difficult client. You helped with a lot of behind the scenes stuff most people don't think about.

I want to thank some of the experts who have helped me with marketing, publicity and book sales, both Marie Swift and Al Martin of Impact Communications, Bob Bly, a great copywriter, and Tom Antion, an internet guru.

I want to give a special recognition to Evan Wolfson, founder of Freedom to Marry. Evan is a modern day civil rights champion. He has supported my efforts from day one by appearing on my radio show and helping promote the book.

I also want to thank all the pre-release readers and reviewers of *Retire Secure! For Same-Sex Couples*. Special thanks go to Ed Slott, CPA and

Jane Bryant Quinn, two high profile finance experts, who provided glowing testimonials. Many more of my colleagues and peers offered thoughtful testimonials. I have included as many as I could. Your support means more to me than I can adequately express.

I must also convey my gratitude to my other full-time employees who provide so much help in my practice that without them, the book could never have been written: They have also been around for a long time, giving both to me personally and to our company great stability: Glenn Venturino, CPA (how can I properly thank you for 26 years of superb service to our clients); Sandy Proto, thank you for 21 years of superb service as office manager (without Sandy the office would cease to function); Alice Davis, 11 years, who is so wonderful and personable with our clients and is the first to jump on board when anything needs to be done; Donna Master, 16 years, who keeps our books, which would certainly be a shambles without her dedicated precision; and Daryl Ross, 15 years, our legal administrative assistant/master tax return compiler who rolls up her sleeves and gets it done year after year. Special thanks to Amanda Cassady-Schweinsberg, our marketing director, who is back on her feet after some extensive surgery. Welcome back, Amanda!

Thanks also to our part-time staff members who make life livable: Bev Patak, Curt Borowski and Diane Markel, CPA (14 years).

Special thanks also go to our joint venture partners who provide the investment arm of the assets-under-management side of our business. Thanks to P.J. DiNuzzo and his team at DiNuzzo Index Advisors, Inc. and Charlie Smith and his team at Fort Pitt Capital Group. We could not do what we do without both of your firms.

There is a special subcontractor who works on my behalf whom I want to thank. Stephen May, my webmaster for 18 years! How can I properly thank you? Stephen did the web work for the first version of www.outestateplanning.com in 2002!

To matters of the heart, a special thanks to my wife, Cindy Lange. She is probably the only women alive who could put up with being married to me. (If you think I am overly being solicitous, just ask my employees; they will confirm that being married to me would be *extremely* difficult, and few could put up with me). Her imprint is on every page of the book. Cindy has been enormously resourceful in many areas and has made both significant direct and indirect contributions to the book. This book would never have happened without her help, support, and love.

Finally, thank you to my 19-year-old daughter, Erica. Erica, is a computer science and engineering student, whom I love dearly. I wish everyone had her open attitude about people of different sexual orientations, race, background, etc.

Thank you all.

Introduction

There were two identically situated same-sex couples: they had the same amount of money, invested identically, and spent identically too. There was only one big difference: the first couple *did not* read *Retire Secure for Same Sex Couples* and plan for their future using our advice, but the second couple did.

The first couple's plan:

1. don't get married

2. take Social Security at age 62

3. don't make Roth IRA conversions

4. don't use our IRA and estate planning strategies (they can't without marrying)

The second couple's plan

1. get married (in a state that recognizes same-sex marriage)*

2. use the "Apply and Suspend" strategy at age 66 for Social Security

3. make a series of Roth IRA conversions

4. use our recommended IRA and estate planning strategies for married couples

Here is the difference in their future finances using reasonable assumptions.**

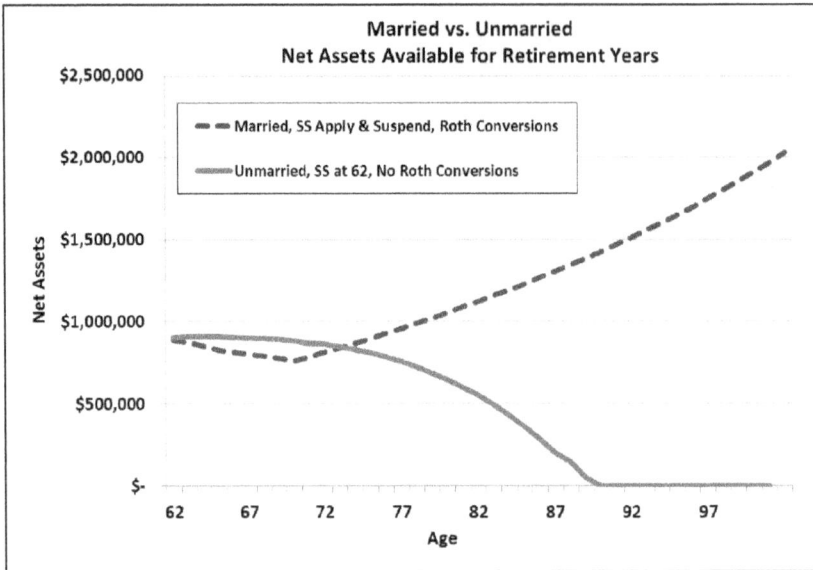

Married vs. Unmarried
Net Assets Available for Retirement Years

Using the proactive strategies explained in this book, our legally married same-sex couple (the blue line) enjoys a comfortable retirement, and still has $1,427,275 at age 90. The unmarried same-sex couple, who didn't take our advice, runs out of money at age 90.

There are fantastic opportunities for same-sex couples to increase their wealth, cut their taxes, and dramatically increase their financial security and the financial security of their surviving spouse/partner. These opportunities are only available because of the new laws on same-sex marriage that were passed in 2013. This is new territory for same-sex couples—finally, you can take advantage of some of the same long-term planning strategies that have always been available to straight couples. But, this also means that you can now make the same mistakes that straight couples frequently make, and some of those mistakes could have disastrous consequences for your surviving partner/spouse.

I wrote this book because I believe it is critical to get this information to everyone in the LGBT community. I am also contributing 100% of all the proceeds that I receive from sales of this book to Freedom to Marry, the premier civil rights group fighting for the legal right for same sex couples to marry. It is headed by Evan Wolfson, a true civil rights champion. If I can influence thousands and preferably hundreds of thousands of people to follow the lead of the married couple in this example, that would be a great thing. There will, however, be two major losers if I am successful in this quest - both the IRS and the Social Security Administration will lose billions of dollars. I don't care. I want the money in your family's pocket—you, your partner/spouse, and (if you have any) your children and grandchildren.

The information in this book will likely have more immediate significance

for same-sex couples aged 60 or older. Let me also be frank about my

agenda. I understand that some same-sex couples desire marriage equality

for love and all the other reasons that people want to get married, while other

couples feel that they don't need a piece of paper to validate their

relationship. But, this book is not about emotions, other than the happy

emotions of having a lot more money – it is about how same-sex couples can significantly increase their *financial security* by getting married and making specific decisions that are only available to them under the law if they are legally married. The difference can be so significant, in fact, that I will say that most committed same-sex couples (where at least one member is age 60 or older) should, either on their own or with an advisor, evaluate whether it makes *financial sense* for them to marry.

The advantage for couples with a combined net worth of more than $1,000,000 can be measured in hundreds of thousands of dollars, sometimes well over $1,000,000 as seen above. For couples with a net worth of less than $1,000,000, the savings will not be as great, but good planning could mean the difference between the surviving partner/spouse being financially secure and living comfortably, versus living out his or her retirement years in poverty. I want to make sure that, no matter what happens to the stock market, and no matter what happens to their partners or spouses—my clients and readers will always have food on the table, shelter over their heads, gas in the car, and a little bit of money for Saturday night. Getting married and taking the appropriate steps can, in many instances, make the difference between being financially secure and not having these basic necessities.

What changed, and why didn't I write this book ten years ago?

A recent tax case, an IRS revenue ruling, and two laws that I believe will soon pass are going to have a significant impact on the financial planning opportunities available for same-sex couples in committed relationships.

What are these changes?

1. The Supreme Court ruling, United States v. Windsor, deeming Section 3 of the Defense of Marriage Act (DOMA) unconstitutional.

2. Revenue Ruling 2013-17, subsequent to the Supreme Court ruling, affected federal income taxes for same-sex couples. This ruling is less well known than the Windsor case, but far more important (financially) to same-sex couples. The biggest impact of the new ruling is on the treatment of IRAs and retirement plans, upon the death of the owner.

3. Proposed changes in the tax law regarding IRAs and retirement plans inherited by a beneficiary other than a spouse. Most IRA experts, including myself, believe that these proposed changes in the law will eventually pass. If they do, they will have a draconian impact on *unmarried* same-sex couples.

4. Inevitable changes in the law regarding same-sex spousal benefits and survivor benefits for Social Security.

In the chapters that follow, I will do my best to explain why I am recommending that many, if not most, 60+-year-old same-sex couples in committed relationships consider entering into a legally valid marriage in a state that recognizes same-sex marriage—even if they return to live in a state that does not recognize their marriage. But let me be absolutely clear: *I am only talking about financial reasons for getting married!*

Each couple's situation is unique, and the information and recommendations that I present might not be appropriate for your situation. The information in the book is not a prescription for every couple; rather, it is meant to open your eyes to possibilities that were not available to same-sex couples prior to the Supreme Court ruling in 2013. Given that caveat, however, I believe the strategies I describe in this book will benefit many, if not most, same-sex couples. And, to give you the complete picture, I will also cover some of the financial downsides of getting married—or, at least, the downsides of getting married in the short term.

I know that many individuals do not have the time or patience to read through all of the details in a financial book. This information is so important to their futures, though, that I felt compelled to prepare a summary version for those folks, that I call "The Essence of the Book Boiled Down to 9 Graphs". If all you want is to know the "answer," and, at least for now, don't care how I arrived at my recommendations, then please enjoy the charts in the next section!

* Even if the state you live in does not recognize same-sex marriage, our strategies will still result in similar financial benefits, assuming that the anticipated changes to Social Security regulations take effect.

** These couples are fictional. But the outcomes are accurate based upon certain reasonable assumptions (covered in detail in Chapter 8).

The Essence of the Book Boiled Down to 9 Graphs

Retire Secure! for Same Sex Couples quantitatively compares various courses of action. For those who don't want to read through the explanation and detail, just looking at the 9 graphs could provide critical information with a minimum of reading effort. Please be aware that the recommendations beneath each figure will be advantageous in most situations, but not for everyone.

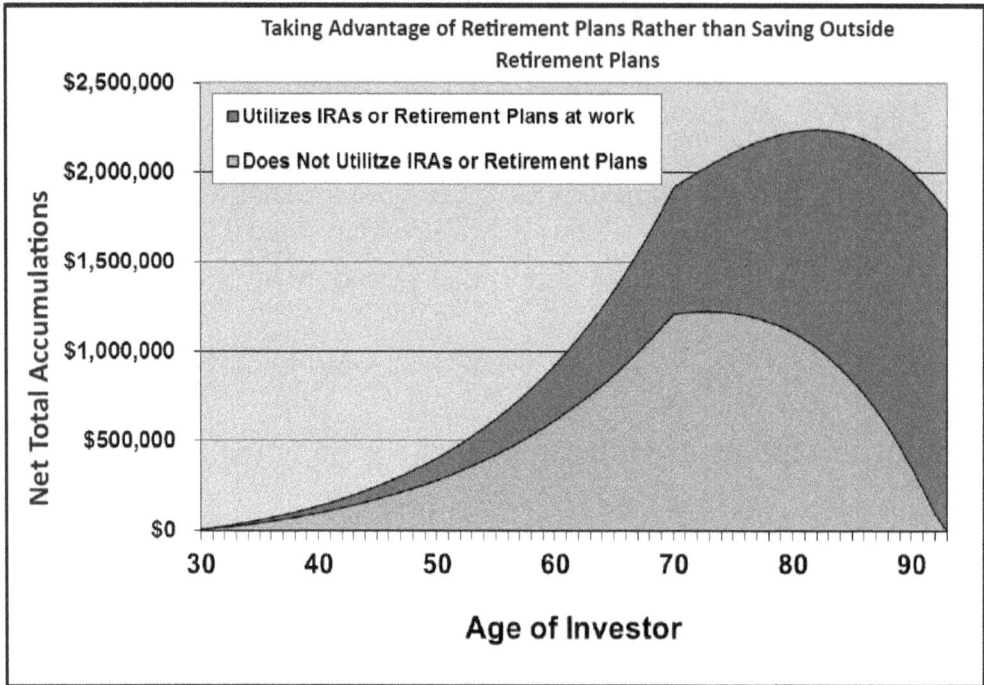

Taking Advantage of Retirement Plans Rather than Saving Outside Retirement Plans

It's better to save in IRAs and retirement plans versus saving in after-tax accounts (regular investments outside IRAs or retirement plans).

This graph shows the total net assets* for two identically situated people, except one contributes to his retirement plan at work and the other saves outside the retirement plan. They each have the same earnings, invest the same out of pocket amount at the same rate, have the same tax bracket, spend the same, etc. The difference is dramatic. The lesson: Don't pay taxes now, pay taxes later—during the accumulation stage while you are working. Please see page 30.

* We measure $100 in an IRA as $75 net assets because there is a $25 income tax associated with the $100 IRA. This applies to this and the following graph.

Benefits of Spending After-Tax Savings before IRAS and Other Retirement Assets

Net Total Accumulations of Retirement Funds and After-Tax Savings

Y-axis values: $0, $200,000, $400,000, $600,000, $800,000, $1,000,000, $1,200,000, $1,400,000, $1,600,000

Legend:
■ Spend After-Tax Funds First
▫ Spend Retirement Funds First

X-axis values: 65, 70, 75, 80, 85

AGE OF INVESTOR

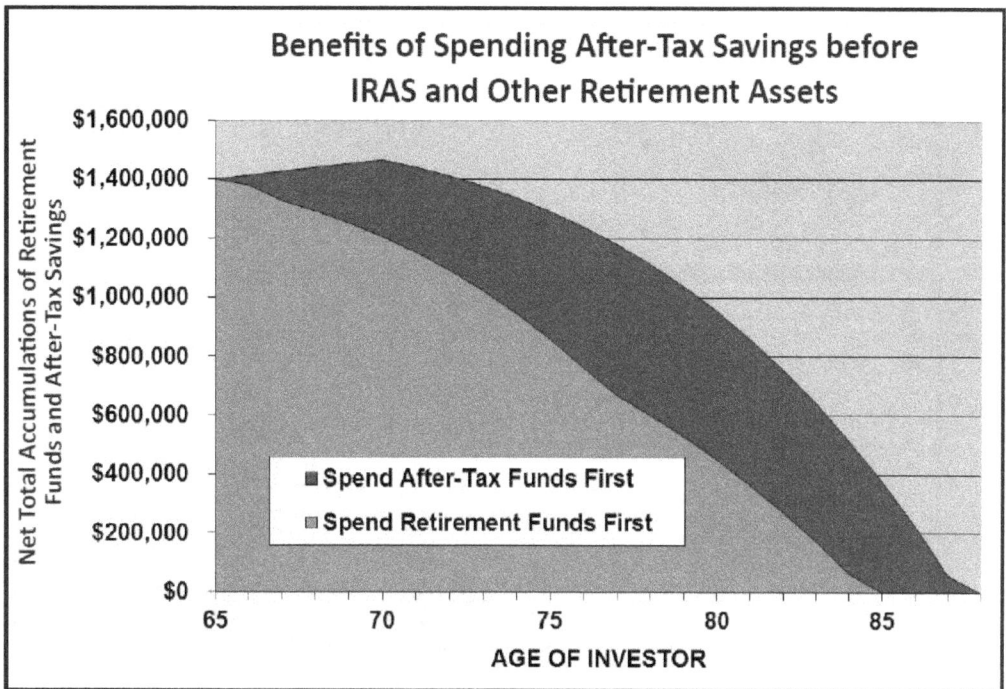

It's generally best to spend assets in this order: 1) after-tax savings 2) traditional IRA and retirement assets.

Of course, at age 70 you will have to take money out of your IRA. Given a choice, however, you should spend your after tax savings first. You will have more money if you keep your money growing tax-deferred for as long as possible. Don't pay taxes now, pay taxes later—when you are retired and in the distribution stage.

Please see page 32.

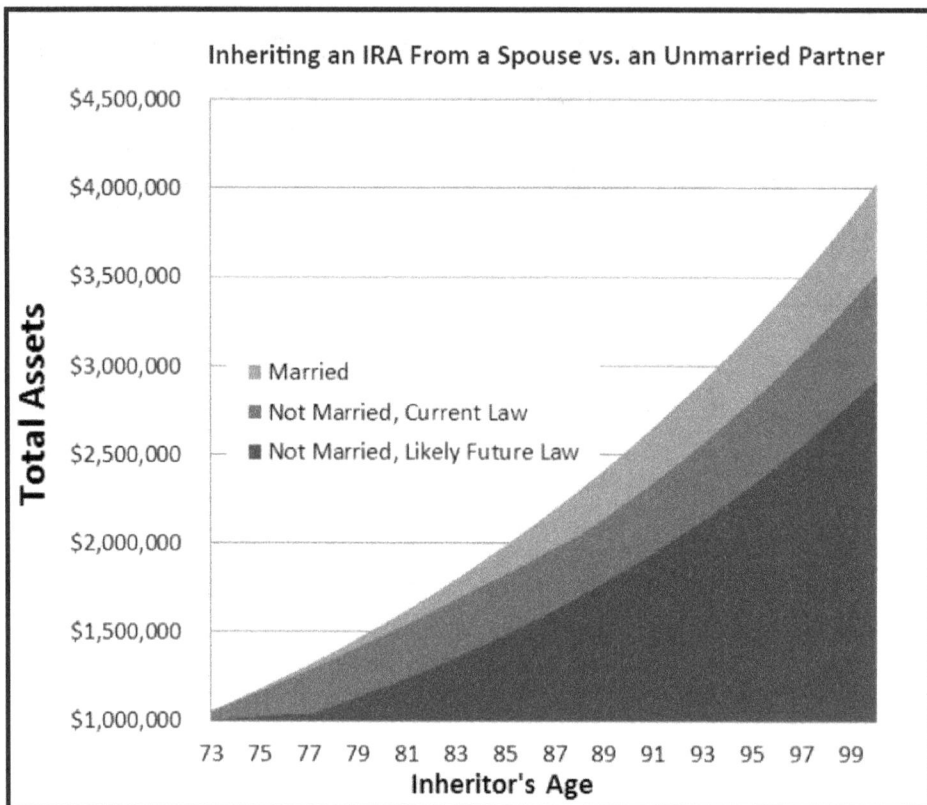

Inheriting an IRA From a Spouse vs. an Unmarried Partner

Estate planning: Get married to provide maximum IRA and retirement plan assets for your partner after your death.

This graph shows the total assets for two individuals who each inherit a $1,000,000 IRA at the age of 72—one inherits from his spouse and the other from his unmarried partner. The tax laws will allow a surviving spouse to keep the money growing tax-deferred much longer than they allow for a surviving partner. Under the projected law changes for *Inherited IRAs*, the scenario is even worse for the unmarried survivor. Getting married allows your surviving spouse to pay taxes later than if you stayed unmarried. Don't pay taxes now, pay taxes later—even after you die.

Please see page 54.

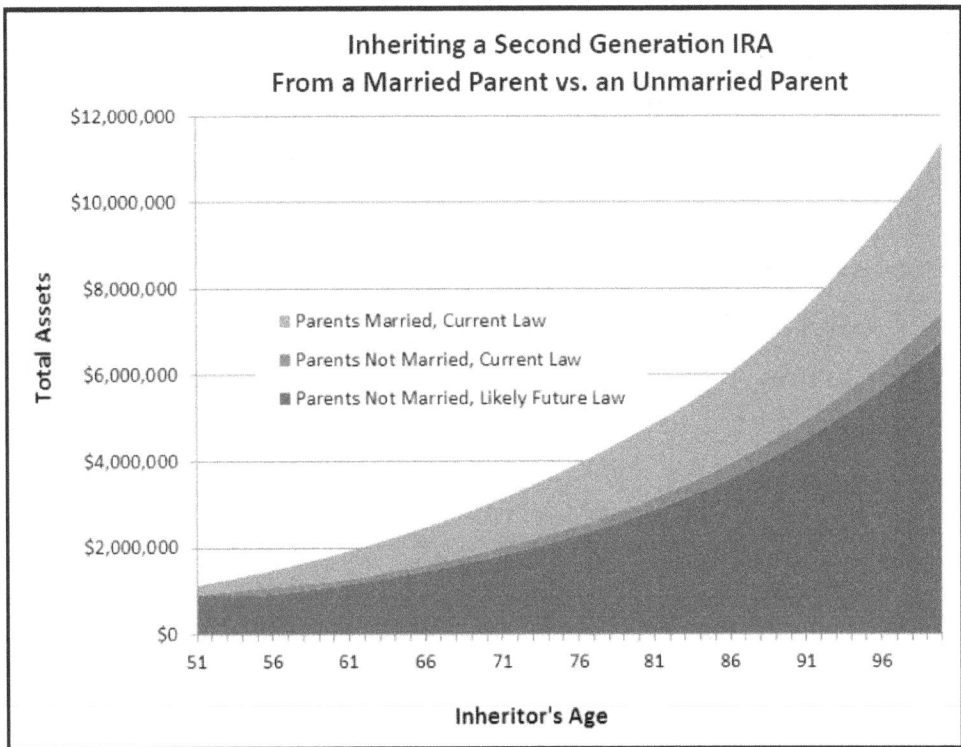

Inheriting a Second Generation IRA
From a Married Parent vs. an Unmarried Parent

Estate planning: Get married to provide maximum assets for your children or other heirs after both you and your partner die.

This graph shows the difference to the eventual heir depending on whether the person leaving him the IRA had married vs. had not gotten married. Tax laws favor the married couple when one of the spouses dies, allowing the surviving spouse to "pay taxes later." In addition to this advantage, tax laws favor heirs of a married couple. When the surviving spouse dies, his heir is permitted to "stretch" the IRA and "pay taxes (much) later."

Tax laws penalize the unmarried couple. The first time an IRA is inherited by a non-spouse, the unmarried partner is forced to "pay taxes sooner." The rules are even less favorable for the surviving partner's heir, forcing him to "pay taxes (much) sooner." Don't pay taxes now, pay taxes later—even after both you and your partner/spouse are gone. Please see page 56.

Starting Social Security Benefits At 62 Years Old vs. 70 Years Old

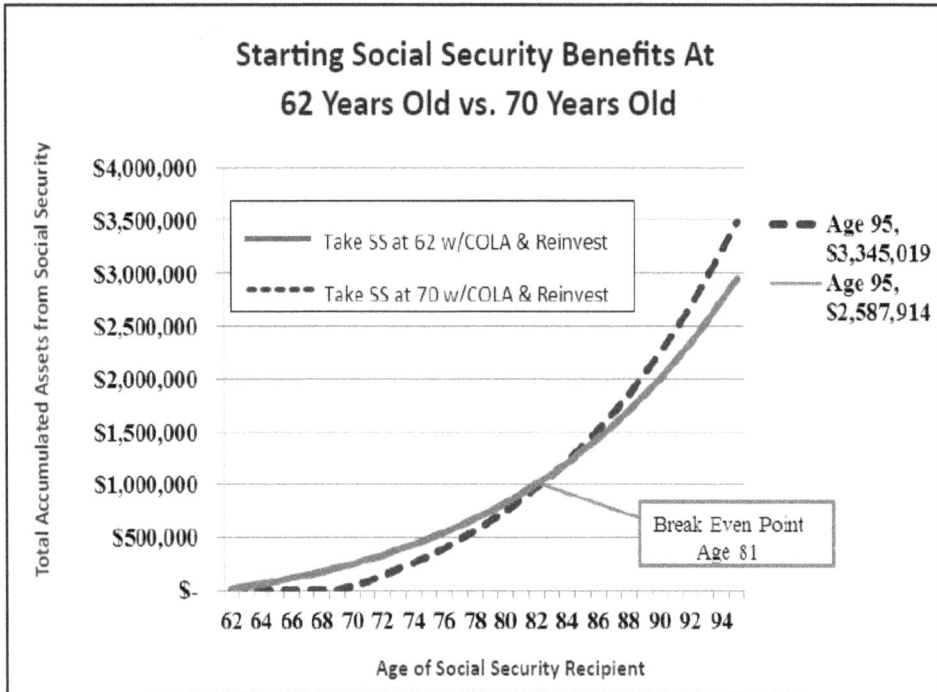

Independent of getting married, it's better to wait until 70 to take Social Security than electing to take Social Security at 62.

The graph shows the total of all Social Security benefits received, plus interest, by two different people with identical earnings records. One begins collecting Social Security at age 62 and the other begins collecting at age 70.

Your benefit will be 76% plus the cost of living adjustment larger if you wait until age 70 to start collecting Social Security, as compared to starting at 62. The longer you live, the more you may need that larger benefit.

Please see page 69.

Unmarried vs. Married Using Apply & Suspend for Social Security

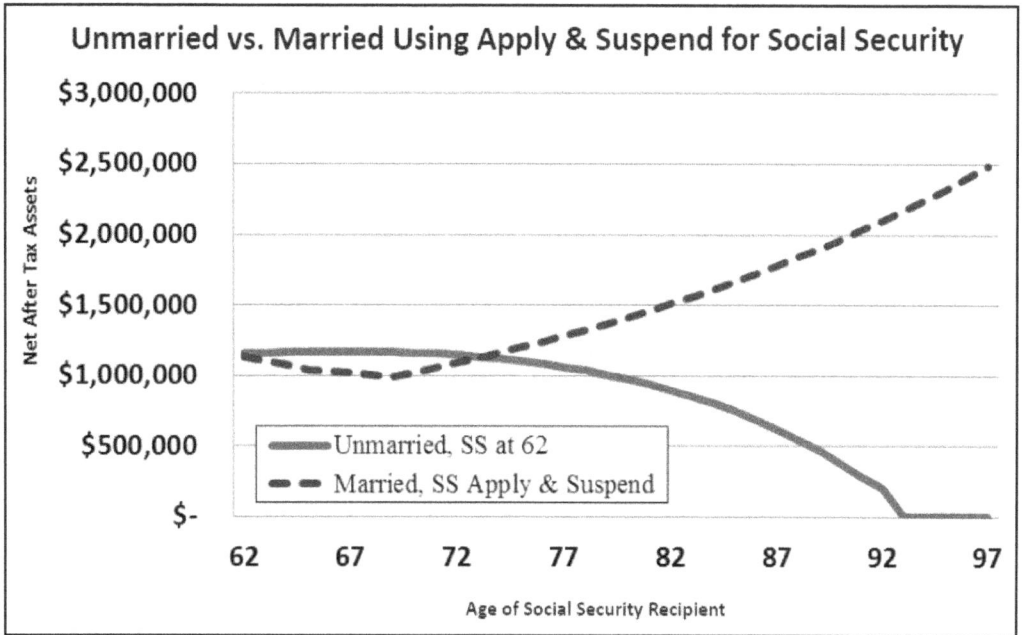

Chart showing Net After Tax Assets (y-axis: $- to $3,000,000) vs. Age of Social Security Recipient (x-axis: 62 to 97). Legend: Unmarried, SS at 62; Married, SS Apply & Suspend.

It's better to "Apply and Suspend" Social Security benefits until age 70.

The graph compares the net total assets for a married couple who uses a technique we often recommend called "Apply and Suspend", to the assets of an unmarried couple who cannot take advantage of that strategy. Both couples start out with the same amount of money, spend the same amount of money and have identical earnings records. In this scenario, none of the individuals die. The unmarried couple runs out of money at age 92, while the married couple's assets are over $2,000,000 and growing.

Please see page 79.

Unmarried vs. Married Using Apply & Suspend for Social Security With an Early Death

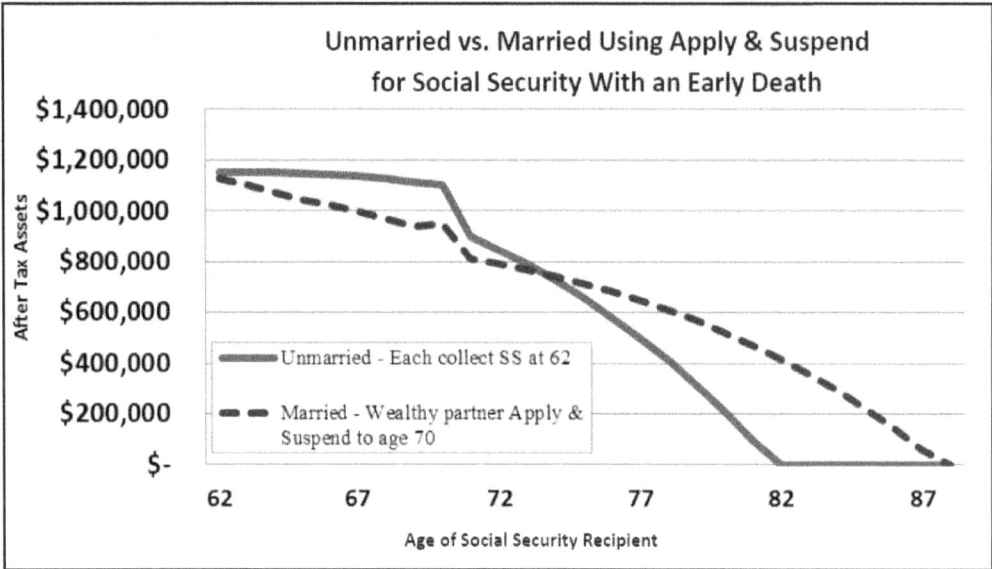

Estate Planning: If the partner/spouse with the stronger earnings record dies first, it's much better for the surviving partner if they had been married and utilized the "Apply and Suspend" strategy.

This graph shows the total after-tax assets for two couples: one married, using the "Apply and Suspend" technique for Social Security benefits, and one unmarried, unable to use that strategy. Both couples start out with the same amount of money, spend the same amount of money and have identical earnings records. At the age of 70, the higher wage earner of the two couples dies. The surviving partner/spouse lives off of their savings and their Social Security benefits. The money lasts longer in the married scenario, mainly because by using the "Apply and Suspend" technique, the partner with the stronger earnings record increased his benefit by waiting, and the survivor is able to collect a much higher Social Security benefit, known as a "spousal survivor benefit," based upon his spouse's wages. Please note if the couple never gets married, they can't use the "Apply and Suspend" technique nor is there a survivor benefit.   Please see page 80.

Following Advice in This Book* vs. Ignoring Advice in This Book**
Assets for Dependent Spouse/Partner
After Death of Higher Wage Earner

Legend:
- Married Current Law
- Not Married, Current Law
- Not Married, Likely Future Law

Y-axis: Net Total Assets
($1,200,000; $1,000,000; $800,000; $600,000; $400,000; $200,000; $-)

X-axis: Inheritor's Age (79, 80, 81, 82, 83, 84, 85, 86, 87, 88, 89, 90, 91)

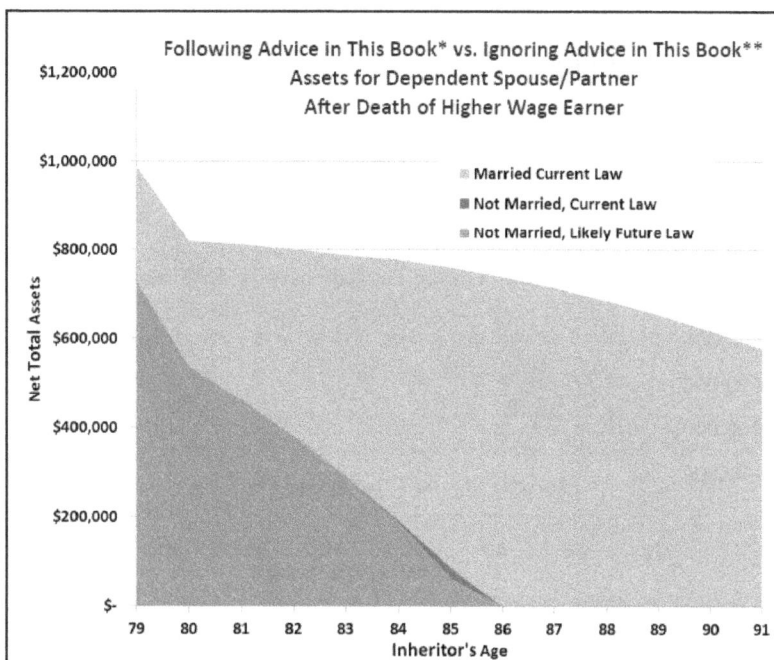

* Following Advice in this Book: Marry, "Apply and Suspend" Social Security, Make Roth IRA Conversions, Take Survivor Social Security Benefits

** Ignoring Advice in this Book: Remain Single, Can't "Apply and Suspend" Social Security, Don't Make Roth IRA Conversions, Can't take Survivor Social Security

Best case scenario for the surviving partner is if the couple gets married, "Applies and Suspends" Social Security to age 70, makes Roth IRA conversions, and takes Spousal Social Security benefits at 66.

The graph shows the total net assets for two people: one who followed all of the advice in this book and one who did not. In this scenario, the higher wage earner dies first at age 78. Because the married couple followed the advice in this book, the couple accumulated $300,000 in additional funds between the ages of 62 and 70, by taking advantage of "Apply and Suspend" for Social Security and by making Roth IRA Conversions. After one spouse dies, the married survivor has further advantages over the unmarried survivor: he can collect higher social security benefits based on his spouse's wages and can leave money in the inherited IRAs and retirement plans growing tax deferred much longer.

Please see page 131.

Adult Child Inherits Assets from Widowed Father

Net Total Assets

$1,800,000
$1,600,000
$1,400,000
$1,200,000
$1,000,000
$800,000
$600,000
$400,000
$200,000
$-

■ Parents Married - Inherited Roth IRA

50   55   60   65   70   75   80   85   90

Inheritor's Age

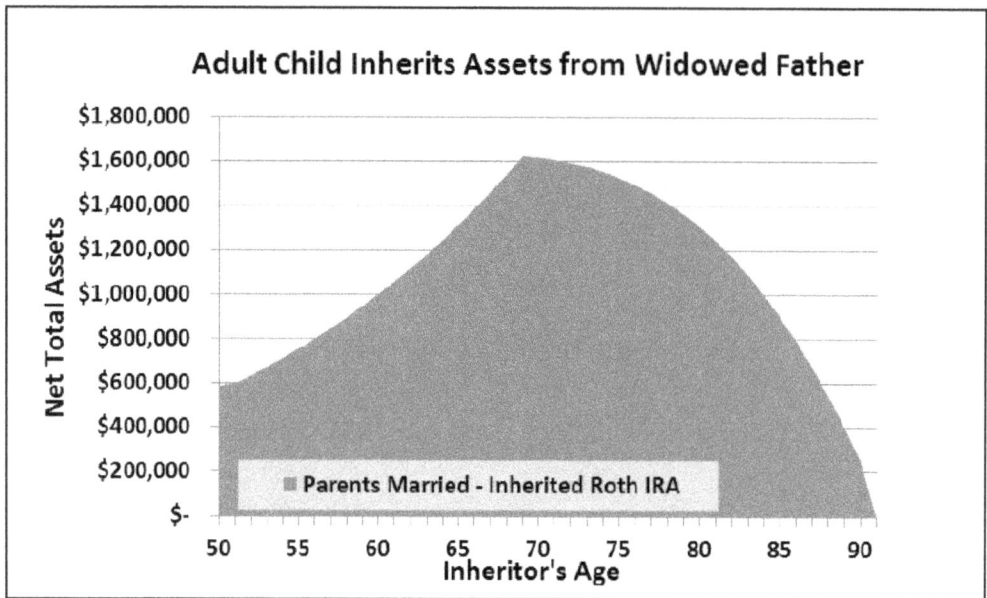

In this example, the only scenario with money available for the next generation inheritance is if the parents married, used the "Apply and Suspend" strategy for Social Security, and optimized Roth IRA conversions. If they didn't get married, took Social Security early, and didn't make any Roth IRA conversions, the adult child doesn't inherit anything.

Please see page 139.

1

The Defense of Marriage Act (DOMA) and the Consequences of the Windsor Decision

Change is the law of life.
And those who look only to the past or present are certain to miss the future.
John F. Kennedy

Main Topics

- What are the effects of the Windsor decision on financial and estate planning?
- Should my partner and I get married to take advantage of these new rules?
- What should I be doing right now?

Key Idea

It might be profitable for committed same-sex couples to entertain the idea of getting legally married in a state that recognizes same-sex marriages. The Windsor decision and its aftermath will have a far-reaching impact on income taxes, inheriting IRAs and retirement plans, and likely Social Security for same-sex couples.

Chapter One Overview

This chapter will offer same-sex couples solid strategies for securing your and your partner's financial future.

We look at the consequences of the Supreme Court decision in United States v. Windsor, which struck down Section 3 of DOMA. You will also learn about a new revenue ruling from the

Internal Revenue Service (IRS) which specifies the difference between "state of celebration" and "state of domicile," and why, in light of all these changes, a legally recognized marriage could alter your finances and financial planning to the better.

United States v. Windsor

The Back-Story

Edith Windsor and Thea Spyer resided in New York. In 2007, after celebrating their 40th anniversary as a committed same-sex couple, they got married in Canada. New York law recognized same-sex marriages performed elsewhere, and the state afforded the couple the same status, responsibilities, and protections of other married people. However, they were not considered "married" under federal law because of the Defense of Marriage Act (DOMA[1]). When Spyer died in 2009, she left her entire estate to Edith

---

[1] DOMA has several sections. Section 2, which was not challenged in the Windsor case, allows states to refuse to recognize same-sex marriages performed under the laws of other states. Section 3, which was disputed and overturned in the Windsor case, applies to the entire United States Code. The original language of Section 3 stated: "In determining the meaning of any Act of Congress, or of any ruling, regulation, or interpretation of the various administrative bureaus and agencies of the United States, the word "marriage" means only a

Windsor. Her estate had a significant federal tax liability; those taxes would have been zero if the federal government had recognized same-sex marriage and afforded those unions the same protections as straight marriages. Edith Windsor sought to claim the unlimited federal marital deduction (which is automatically given to the surviving spouse of a straight couple) on Thea's federal estate tax return—thus challenging the federal government to recognize her Canadian marriage as the state of New York had recognized it. In 2010, the IRS notified Windsor that it disallowed the estate's claim for a refund on the grounds that the surviving spouse was not a spouse as defined by DOMA. Windsor then filed a suit in federal court challenging Section 3 of DOMA and won.

---

legal union between one man and one woman as husband and wife, and the word "spouse" refers only to a person of the opposite sex who is a husband or wife." This meant that, even if you were a legally married same-sex couple in a state that recognizes same-sex marriages, the federal government would not recognize your marriage for any purpose. The decision in United States v. Windsor is a landmark case which held that DOMA created an "unequal subset of state-sanctioned marriages…depriving some couples married under the laws of their State, but not others, of both rights and responsibilities, creating two contradictory marriage regimes within the same State. It also forced same-sex couples to live as married for the purposes of state law but unmarried for the purpose of federal law." The case was brought forward by Edith Windsor.

The Supreme Court Ruled DOMA Unconstitutional Because of Unequal Treatment in the Federal Estate Tax

The Supreme Court held that Section 3 of DOMA is unconstitutional as a deprivation of the liberty of the person protected by the Fifth Amendment to the Constitution and found Section 3 of the statute to be invalid and in violation of the Fifth Amendment. The ruling was limited to lawful marriages.

While the Windsor case dealt only with estate taxes, the holding that Section 3 is unconstitutional, and the aftermath of that ruling, has already had an enormous impact on income taxes, IRAs and retirement plans, and potentially (likely, as things are already under review) Social Security for legally married same-sex couples.

Internal Revenue Service Extends the Windsor Decision in Revenue Ruling 2013-17

On August 29, 2013, the U.S. Department of the Treasury and the Internal Revenue Service ruled that same-sex couples who are legally married in states and other countries that recognize their marriage, *will be treated as married for federal income tax purposes*. The ruling applies *regardless* of whether the couple lives in a state that recognizes same-sex marriage, or in a state that does not recognize same-sex marriage. The revenue ruling extends the federal income tax aspects of the Windsor decision. Under the ruling, same-sex couples will be treated as married for all federal tax purposes, including income, gift, and estate taxes.

The Revenue Ruling 2013-17, located at http://www.irs.gov/pub/irs-drop/rr-13-17.pdf, concludes that for federal tax purposes, the words "spouse" and "marriage" include same-sex couples if they are lawfully married under state law. For federal purposes, the law of the state in which the marriage took place, also known as the "state of celebration," defines the marriage status, even if the couple resides in a non-recognition state. As of this writing, that includes Pennsylvania and, there are a total of 33 non-recognition states.

Any same-sex marriage *legally* entered into in one of the states that currently recognize same-sex marriages is covered by Revenue Ruling 2013-17. In order for a marriage to be considered legal by the Federal government, the marriage had to have taken place in a state or country that has legalized same-sex marriages. As of this writing, 17 jurisdictions in the US (including individual states and the District of Columbia) have done so. The revenue ruling is crucial for inherited IRAs and retirement plans, and it simplifies the income tax filing status for same-sex married couples. The ruling also opens the door for changes in spousal and survivor benefits for Social Security purposes for residents of non-recognition states.

The State of Celebration vs. the State of Domicile

The "state of celebration" refers to the state in which the marriage took place. The "state of domicile" refers to where you live. Using the *state of celebration* as the criteria for recognizing a same-sex marriage for federal purposes means that as long as you are married in a state (or a country) that recognizes same-sex marriage, even if you *live* in a state that doesn't recognize same-sex marriage (like Pennsylvania), you will be given the same federal tax advantages as straight married couples.

My "Eureka!" Moment

When the federal government decided to use the state of celebration rather than the state of domicile to determine who is married, I said, "Ah ha! Now we have a real opportunity to dramatically cut taxes and increase financial security for almost all same-sex couples who are willing to get married and take my financial recommendations." With my specialized knowledge of IRAs, retirement plans and Social Security, I knew that most same-sex couples would not fully appreciate these new opportunities. So, I appointed myself the educator and messenger of these extremely significant opportunities. And I am telling you that if you are in a committed same-sex relationship and at least one of you is 60 or older, for federal tax purposes and Social Security purposes, it might very well behoove you to run off and get married in a state that recognizes same-sex marriage. And you can still return to live in the state where you are living now! Let me make it perfectly clear: same-sex couples who live in any of the 33 non-recognition states might want to consider getting married in New York or any of the recognition states, and then come back home to resume their lives in their state that doesn't recognize same-sex marriage.[2]

If you are a *legally* married same-sex couple, then the revenue ruling will apply to you and your spouse no matter which state you live in. It is a very, very big deal. In the following two chapters, we quantify the financial differences between getting married and taking my advice, versus maintaining the status quo. The difference could be life changing. I knew I

---

[2] This book is not meant to be a scholarly treatise on the Windsor case or even the legal right of same-sex couples to marry. Earlier drafts had legal analysis that constitutional lawyers could read and still argue about. Rather, this book is meant to give practical advice to same-sex couples on how to optimize their finances. That said, one reviewer, a gay law professor who thinks and writes on gay issues, warned that Windsor and the revenue ruling still do require a "valid marriage". The reviewer questioned whether a same-sex couple that resides in Pennsylvania and crosses the border to New York and gets married appropriately following New York state law and returns to Pennsylvania has a "valid marriage" that would satisfy the case, the revenue ruling and presumably additional changes to follow. I clearly think it does and so does every attorney and every authority I know except this one attorney. I feel compelled to say there may be an argument that marriage in that circumstance isn't a "valid marriage," but I discount that
possibility so strongly that I am going to ignore it for my recommendations.

could make a crucial impact on thousands, perhaps hundreds of thousands of people. To be fair, I am not a saint. I also figured it would be profitable for me in the long run. But, what really spurred me to write this book was knowing that this opportunity for same-sex couples to get married and enjoy enormous financial benefits doesn't just apply to California or New York or other states that recognize same-sex marriage residents. It applies to every same-sex couple in the U.S. who is willing to get married and implement the strategies that I recommend, including those who live in Pennsylvania, where I live and practice.

Other financial experts who truly understand IRAs, retirement plans, and Social Security will be coming along and giving similar advice. The IRS ruling is especially critical for IRA and retirement plan owners. But, if the Social Security Administration or Congress or the courts change the rules for Social Security to mirror the IRS changes, it will be even more important. As of this moment, the Acting Commissioner of the Social Security Administration has not said that Social Security benefits for same-sex couples will be determined based on state of celebration; they still use the *state of residence for this*. But I (and virtually every knowledgeable person I speak to about this matter) believe it is only a matter of time before that law will take effect.

So, regardless of when your state finally legalizes same-sex marriage, we anticipate that, at the federal level, the Social Security Administration will adopt the "state of celebration" criteria for determining spousal benefits. And, that might be the most compelling reason—even more than the income tax reasons related to IRAs and retirement plans—to get legally married. In the event that the financially-stronger spouse dies first, their strong Social Security benefit will not die with them—and that offers considerable financial protection for the surviving spouse. Without marriage, the surviving partner gets nothing. This might not seem important to you now, but when you look at the numbers in Chapter 3, it will really hit home.

As of right now, if you're a Pennsylvania resident, or reside in any of the other 33 states not recognizing same-sex marriage, you cannot get spousal benefits for Social Security. If you are a New York resident or a resident of one of the other recognition states, then you can get spousal Social Security benefits. Not only is that unfair, it's an administrative nightmare! This is why most knowledgeable professionals feel that it's just a matter of time before there will be a change similar to the one that the IRS made saying that, as long as you have a legal marriage entered into in a state that recognizes same-sex marriages, you will be eligible for spousal and survivor benefits.

Pennsylvania and Other States That Don't Recognize Same-Sex Marriage

> *Newt Gingrich says he does not support gay marriage. He says marriage is a sacred sacrament that should only be between a man and his first, second, and third wives.*
>
> **- Conan O'Brien**

Pennsylvania and other states have some funny rules. One Pennsylvania law that makes most people scratch their heads is this: same-sex couples who are legally married in a state that *does* recognize same-sex marriages, and who are Pennsylvania residents, must file their federal tax return as "married"—but their state tax return as "single." That's stupid, but that's the way it is right now. In addition, you can't name your spouse as your spouse on a death certificate. There is a 15% inheritance tax for same-sex couples whether they are legally married or not. (As a comparison, the inheritance tax is *zero* for straight couples, and the rate is 4.5% for children.) The discrimination against same-sex couples is unfair and deserves to be overturned in Pennsylvania and elsewhere with similar laws. We're hoping that it is going to change, but Pennsylvania is so extreme that it is currently treating the spouses of a legally married same-sex couple as though they are not even related to one another. Other states have some peculiar rules, too. Ohio recognizes same-sex marriages only for purposes of the death certificate. Although Colorado bans same-sex marriages, the state allows civil unions, and provides limited recognition of same-sex unions for designated beneficiary agreements. Oregon bans same-sex marriages, but domestic partnerships are allowed, and the state recognizes same-sex marriages from out of state. Wisconsin bans same-sex marriages but allows domestic partnerships, and the state permits same-sex couples in a domestic partnership to inherit from their partner without a will and take family medical leave. As you might imagine, the issue of same-sex marriage is being hotly litigated in Pennsylvania and in many other states. I could be wrong, but I think we have a pretty good chance when it comes to recognizing same-sex marriages, at least in Pennsylvania. Clearly, we need to have some consistency!

The federal tax laws can also be "interesting". Did you know that, if you are legally married now, you have the option to go back and amend your federal tax returns for the past three years – even though the IRS did not make their ruling until 2013? It would be smart to run the numbers to see if it will be favorable to file amended returns as *married filing joint* instead of *single* (a lot more on that later in Chapter 4). Also, if your spouse died and you paid federal estate tax because your marriage was not recognized at that time, you can now go back and file an amended estate tax return.

Tying the Knot or Not: Financial Considerations for Same-Sex Couples

So, if financial considerations weigh into your decision to get married, does it make sense to get married? Now, don't get all excited about the federal estate tax because if you don't have more than five million dollars, and are not likely to grow your estate to five million dollars, the estate tax implications of the Windsor case are probably not relevant. But for IRA owners, pension participants, and retirement plan owners, the financial implications of getting married are enormous. The ability to enjoy spousal benefits for Social Security will also be enormously important for residents of states that recognize same-sex marriages. Hopefully, down the line, residents of the non-recognition states will be able to enjoy those benefits too.

But, there are also financial reasons why you might NOT want to get married. For many taxpayers, your income taxes could actually increase if you get married. This is because of the so called "marriage penalty" that currently hurts many straight couples. The marriage penalty means that if you get married, you're going to end up paying more income taxes than you would have if you had both filed single, which is bad. On the flip side, there is also a marriage bonus, which could mean that you will pay less in taxes, which is good. Chapter 4 examines the circumstances under which your marriage is more likely to result in an income tax penalty or an income tax bonus for federal tax purposes.

You also have to be aware of all of the financial implications of getting married. I counseled one couple that is choosing not to get married now because the financially dependent partner can get cheap health insurance through the Affordable Health Care Act, but they would lose that opportunity if they got married. Their plan is actually to wait until the financially weaker spouse qualifies for Medicare and then get married. That might work out well, or it could be disastrous if the financially stronger spouse dies within the next four years. Only time will tell if it was a

"penny wise and pound foolish" decision. For the purposes of this book and for what we do in practice, we like to "run the numbers" to get a more accurate picture of the advantages and disadvantages of getting married, and we apply our advice in a number of related areas. There will be plenty of "number running" results in future chapters. (For more information on how marriage could affect your health care options, please see Chapter 6.)

As the Legal Landscape Changes, What Should You Do?

The issue of marriage equality is in constant flux. In light of the shifting legal landscape, it seems that the best course of action for same-sex couples who are contemplating marriage is to educate yourselves on your options, and the advantages and disadvantages of different strategies. For most participants in a committed long-term same-sex relationship, particularly if at least one person in the couple is in their sixties or older, getting married and taking our advice on related topics could be extremely profitable for you and your partner/spouse.

Though specific advice has to be made on a case-by-case basis, here are a few action points that same-sex couples in Pennsylvania, or couples in other states that do not recognize same-sex marriage, should consider.

1. If you want to get married (despite all the risks and problems of traditional marriages), travel to a state where marriage equality exists and tie the knot! Of course, consider the risks first – alimony, child support and equitable distribution of property are just as painful for same-sex as straight divorcees. We recommend considering such unpleasant, but often necessary, legal documents like prenuptial agreements and other property agreements. Like Craig Ferguson, a California judge put it—"Congratulations gay people—you are about to discover the joys of alimony." While being legally married will not help residents of states that do not recognize same-sex marriage with regard to their state laws and state tax issues (or to federal laws that defer to the state laws), it will offer benefits for federal estate taxes and for income tax purposes in the IRA world. But, beware! In many situations, marriage does have potentially financially harmful consequences for federal income taxes. Please see Chapter 4 for specifics.

2. Apply for spousal and survivor Social Security benefits when, after reviewing the entire picture, you and/or your trusted advisor feels it is

appropriate. Currently, the Social Security Administration is urging same-sex couples to apply regardless of the legality of their marriage in their state—even couples with civil unions or registered domestic partnerships are encouraged to apply. The Social Security Administration indicated that if changes are made to allow benefits for these partnerships, the administration would backdate benefits to the date of filing. Caution must be exercised in applying for Social Security benefits for same-sex couples, just as for straight couples. We often recommend waiting to apply for Social Security in order to receive higher benefits in later years (see Chapter 3). The uncertainty of the law for same-sex couples makes Social Security planning even more complex, so cases should be examined individually.

3. Act now to prepare or amend your wills and trusts to include special provisions regarding the disbursement of your assets. Your wills and trusts should be consistent with current laws, but include special provisions in case same-sex marriage later becomes legalized in your state, before the time of your or your spouse's death.

4. Discuss advance healthcare directives with your spouse and advisors. It is the right of every American to have an advance health care directive, and hospitals are supposedly obligated to honor them when they are

appropriately drafted and legally binding. Although filling out the appropriate paperwork is no guarantee your wishes will be carried out, it does significantly increase your chances.

5. It is often prudent to pre-plan your funeral arrangements. In many instances, partners in same-sex relationships who aren't considered legally married in the state where they reside have no say in how their deceased loved ones are laid to rest. In Pennsylvania, a simple legal document known as a Statement of Contrary Intent may be prepared, and arrangements can be made with funeral directors to give same-sex couples the right to carry out the wishes of their departed loved ones. Other states that do not recognize same-sex marriage may have similar provisions in their laws as well.

6. Technically, because Section 3 of DOMA was found to be unconstitutional, the statute is deemed to have been invalid from the outset. This means that same-sex couples who were married legally, in a jurisdiction that allows for same-sex marriage, have *always* been legally married according to the federal government. Therefore, those same-sex married couples who would have paid less in federal taxes had they filed jointly, or who could have claimed a marital deduction upon the death of their spouse, now have grounds to file an amended return. Generally, the IRS allows a

taxpayer to file an amended return three years from the date the return was filed or two years from the date the tax was paid, whichever is later. Have a discussion as soon as possible with your CPA or tax attorney about taking advantage of this ruling. However, understand that filing an amended return is optional. Because of the so-called "marriage penalty", some couples might actually owe additional taxes to the IRS for previous years if they file amended returns reflecting a married status. If that is the case, they are not required to file an amended return. A conversation with your tax advisor, followed by a tax assessment for "married filing jointly" vs. "two single taxpayers" would determine which course of action is best for you. Then, depending on the result, either you or your CPA could file amended returns and request a refund. In addition, for tax year 2013 and thereafter, and for taxpayers filing an original tax return on or after September 16, 2013, same-sex married couples generally must file as either married filing separately or married filing jointly.

7. Same-sex couples who are legally married will be treated as married for all federal tax purposes, including income, estate, and gift tax purposes. This applies to all federal tax provisions where being married is a factor, including but not limited to: filing status, personal and dependency exemptions, employee benefits, and the ability to contribute to an IRA (or

Roth IRA) for you and your spouse, even if your spouse doesn't work. A

qualified retirement plan must treat a same-sex spouse as a spouse. Same-sex

spouses are now able to rollover (though technically we prefer a trustee to

trustee transfer) their deceased spouse's benefits into their own IRA,

enabling them to receive benefits over their lifetime and to delay minimum

required distributions (MRD) until age 70½. This means that all of your

existing IRA and retirement plan beneficiary forms should be reviewed,

keeping the new interpretation in mind. Under appropriate circumstances, the

financially stronger spouse and/or the spouse closer to death, should consider

making gifts to his or her spouse in order to avoid state estate taxes. For

more wealthy couples, consider large gifts to take advantage of the unlimited

federal marital gift deduction, which could save huge sums in state

inheritance taxes. (Please see Chapter 7).

8.   Consider purchasing life insurance to protect your spouse and to cover

any transfer taxes (inheritance taxes) incurred by your spouse upon your

death, if your state does not legalize same-sex marriage in your lifetime. Life

and long-term care insurance can help protect your assets and keep you and

your spouse in charge of your money and your future. One particularly

useful insurance tool for same-sex couples is a combination life and long-

term care insurance policy that will cover the costs of long-term care during your life, and pay out what you don't use of the coverage as a death benefit. Life insurance is typically paid to a named beneficiary, and beneficiary designations bypass probate, allowing you to control those funds directly. Depending upon the laws of your state, this strategy may also be used in other non-recognition states with regard to transfer taxes incurred by your spouse upon your death. Life insurance is even more useful for protecting you and your partner if you choose not to marry. Last but not least, life insurance is usually exempt from estate, inheritance and income tax.

It is best to get qualified legal and tax advice to protect and preserve your assets, as well as to protect the rights and interests of your surviving spouse. Establishing a relationship with a trusted advisor can help you pave the way to your goals, both in the current legal environment, and into the future, as the law evolves.

In addition, please consider other potential problems if the marriage doesn't work out. An increasing problem for same-sex married couples who live in states that do not recognize their marriage is the inability to obtain a divorce. Some of the inherent difficulties for couples who are unable to divorce include being legally responsible for each other's debt, the requirement to file federal tax returns as married, removing a spousal beneficiary from a retirement plan, and issues regarding spousal support and the division of marital property.

All states have residency requirements for divorce, but some states have carved out legal exceptions for same-sex couples who were married in that state. The laws in California, Delaware, Hawaii, Illinois, Minnesota, Vermont and the District of Columbia permit same-sex couples who were married in the state to get a divorce in the state even if the couple does not currently reside in the state. Canadian law also permits same-sex couples who married in Canada to get divorced in Canada without having to reside in the country.

> While getting information from a book is great, most readers are best served by establishing a relationship with a good fiduciary advisor. (Which means they have the legal obligation to put your interest ahead of their own.) If you don't have a trusted advisor and can't find anyone that you feel has the appropriate expertise in financial matters as they relate to same-sex couples, there is another option for a limited number of readers. If you are interested in working with me and/or my firm one on one, please visit www.OutEstatePlanning.com/workwithjim or refer to the end of the book for contact information.

2

Optimizing IRAs & Retirement Plans for Same-Sex Couples

A man has made at least a start on discovering the meaning
of human life when he plants shade trees under which he
knows full well he will never sit.

Elton Trueblood (1900–1994)

Main Topics

• What is the difference between inheriting an IRA or retirement plan from my partner vs. my spouse?

• Why beneficiaries should continue to withdraw the least possible amount (the required minimum distribution) out of an IRA they inherit from either a spouse, or as the non-spouse beneficiary of an *Inherited IRA*?

Key Idea

The benefits of marriage are so significant for inheriting IRAs and retirement plans, committed same-sex couples should consider getting married to financially protect their surviving spouse, and even subsequent generations.

Overview of IRAs and Retirement Plans

Life changing opportunities that have only existed for straight couples are now available for same-sex couples—but only if you get married and take the appropriate action. The difference between getting married and taking

appropriate action vs. not getting married could mean the difference between

financial security for the surviving partner, and a life of financial struggle.

Background: The Power of Retirement Plans While Working

In the first two editions of my book *Retire Secure! Pay Taxes Later* (Wiley,

2006 and 2009) I go to great lengths to prove that, in general, it makes sense

to pay taxes later (except when it comes to Roth IRAs and Roth IRA

conversions). The basic premise is that while you are working, you should

contribute the maximum you are permitted to contribute to your retirement

plan (or a combination of retirement plans). That's a form of paying taxes

later because, with a deductible IRA, a 401(k), or other type of retirement

plan, you and/or your employer make tax-deductible contributions. In other

words, you don't pay the taxes on the contributions until you withdraw the

money during your retirement. There are many other ways to delay paying

taxes, and we will cover some of those as well. But for now, to illustrate the

strength of my argument, please take a look at the graph below. It represents

two individuals, Mr. Pay Taxes Later, and Mr. Pay Taxes Now. They are

identical in all respects except for one fundamental difference in their

investment strategy:

- Both men begin investing at age 30.

- Neither of the companies they work for match their contributions. (This is just to simplify the calculation. Adding in employer matching makes the argument even stronger.)

- In 2014, they each start saving $8,000 per year, indexed for inflation.

However,

- Mr. Pay Taxes Later has his entire $8,000 withheld from his paycheck and deposited to his tax-deferred 401(k). (The analysis would be identical if he contributed the money to a traditional deductible IRA, though $8,000 is well over the current allowed IRA contribution.)

- Mr. Pay Taxes Now chooses to not have any retirement funds withheld from his paycheck. He pays income taxes on his full wages, including the $8,000 he chose to not contribute to his retirement plan. He has to pay income tax immediately on the $8,000. After the 25% income tax is paid, he has only 75% of the $8,000, or $6,000, left to invest.

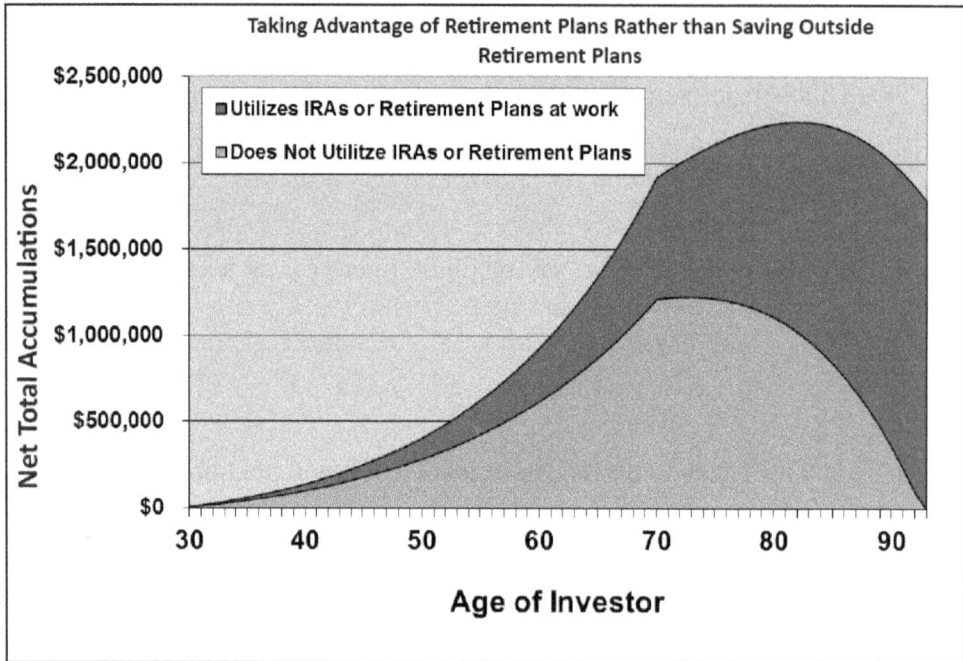

Taking Advantage of Retirement Plans Rather than Saving Outside Retirement Plans

The assumptions for this graph include the following:

1. We use a conservative investment rate of return of 6%, including 70% capital appreciation, with 15% portfolio turnover rate, 15% dividend income, and 15% interest income.

2. Mr. Pay Taxes Later makes retirement savings contributions of $8,000 per year. Mr. Pay Taxes Now invests 25% less due to taxes. Both amounts are indexed for 2.5% annual raises, starting at age 30 until age 70.

3. Starting at age 71, spending from both investors' accounts is equal to the required minimum distributions (RMDs) from Mr. Pay Taxes Later's retirement plan, less related income taxes.

4. Mr. Pay Taxes Later withdraws only the required minimum distribution (RMD), pays the 25% income tax due on his distribution, and spends the rest. Mr. Pay Taxes Now spends the same amount, plus he pays income taxes due on his interest, dividends and realized capital gains.

5. Ordinary tax rates are 25%.

6. Capital gains tax rates are 15%.

7. Dividends are taxed as capital gains.

Now, to be fair, Mr. Pay Taxes Later will have to pay taxes eventually. When he is retired, for every dollar he wants to withdraw he has to take out $1.33. He pockets the dollar and pays $0.33 in taxes (25% of $1.33). If Mr. Pay Taxes Now withdraws a dollar, subject to some capital gains taxes, it's all his. At age 92, however, Mr. Pay Taxes Now has depleted his funds entirely, whereas Mr. Pay Taxes Later has $1,941,727 left in his retirement plan. Given reasonable assumptions and all things being equal, following the adage "Don't pay taxes

now—pay taxes later" can be worth almost $2 million over your lifetime.

Readers interested in more detailed information on the accumulation as well as the distribution phase of IRAs and retirement plans should read my book, *Retire Secure! Pay Taxes Later* (Wiley, 2009)

Background: Which Dollars Should You Spend First in Retirement?

Now, to continue the *pay taxes later* theme, let's look at which dollars you should spend first, after you retire.

When you retire, if you have money outside IRAs and retirement plans, I want you to spend your after-tax dollars *first*, before your IRA or retirement plan dollars. If you can afford it, I don't want you to take any distributions from your IRA or retirement plan until you have to—after age 70½ —when you must begin to take required minimum distributions (RMD). By taking only the required minimum distributions, you keep more of your money growing tax-deferred. That is another form of paying taxes later. If you spend your IRA dollars, you have to pay taxes now.

This graph below is similar to the previous graph except that it represents the distribution phase, not the accumulation phase. This graph shows the difference between two identically situated people with identical investments, tax rates, etc. except one chooses to spend their after tax dollars first (pay taxes later) and the other chooses to spend his IRA or retirement plan first (pay taxes now).

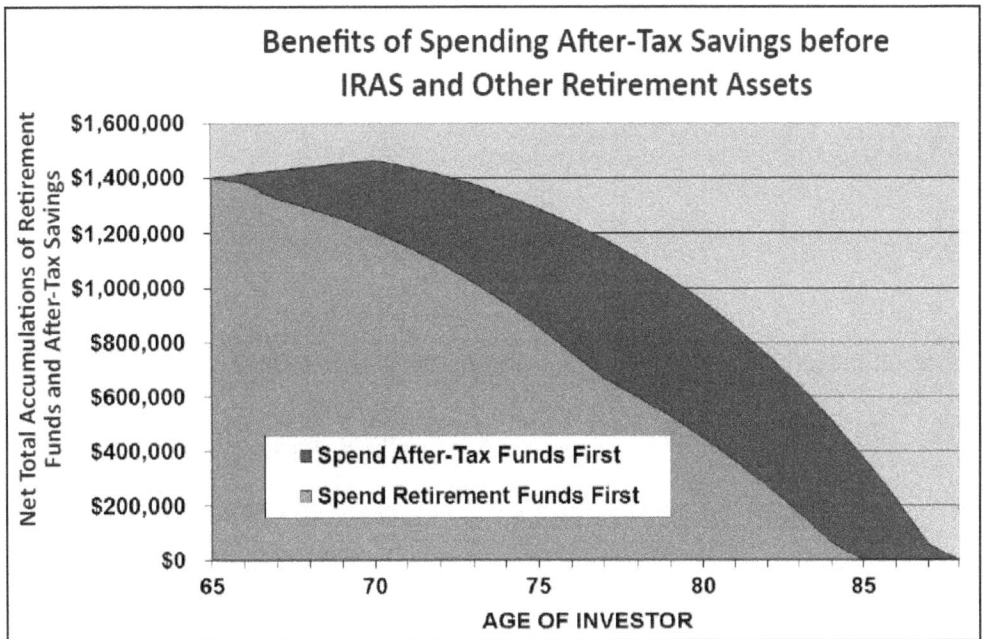

The assumptions for this graph include the following:

1. An investment rate of return of 6%

2. Rate of inflation is 3%

3. Starting at age 65, both investors spend $96,000 per year.

4. Starting at age 65, both investors have beginning After Tax Funds of $300,000 and beginning retirement funds of $1,100,000.

5. Both investors receive $30,000 per year in Social Security benefits adjusted annually for cost of living allowances, but have no other income.

The quantifiable advantage of "paying taxes later" is shown above and, depending on what time period you are measuring, that difference (depending on which dollars you spend first) can be hundreds of thousands of dollars.

The Impact of Marriage on the Accumulation Years

While you are still working, you shouldn't pass up the opportunity to

contribute the maximum allowable to your retirement plans. Marriage may

afford you additional possibilities to contribute that may not be available to you as an unmarried individual; on the other hand, marriage might also eliminate possibilities to contribute.

One advantage of marriage comes into play if one member of the couple is not working. This is relevant because you must have earned income to contribute to any IRA, including a Roth IRA. If a couple is not married, and one partner is not working, that non-working partner will not be allowed to contribute to an IRA or a Roth IRA. However, if the couple marries, the non-working spouse would be able to contribute to an IRA or Roth IRA based upon their working spouse's income. Marriage makes it possible for the couple to put more money in the tax-deferred or tax-free environment. For example, consider the couple Anne and Susan. In 2014, Anne earns $150,000 per year and is not covered by a retirement plan at work. Susan is not working outside the home. If they are unmarried, Anne can contribute to an IRA, but Susan has no earned income and cannot. If they marry, then both Anne and Susan can each contribute $5,500 ($6,500 if they are age 50 or older) to their respective IRAs.

When it comes to Roth IRAs, there is a potential benefit if your income is too high for you to be eligible to make a full Roth IRA contribution. These income limits are different for married and unmarried individuals (refer to table below). You may find that your income is too high for you to make a

Roth IRA contribution as an unmarried taxpayer, but you are able to make a contribution as a married taxpayer. For example, consider Anne and Susan again. In 2014, if they are unmarried, neither Anne nor Susan can contribute to their Roth IRAs. Anne earns above the maximum of $129,000 for a single taxpayer and Susan has no earned income. If Anne and Susan marry, then their combined income of $150,000 is under the $181,000 limit for married couples, so they are both permitted to make the *maximum* allowable contributions to their Roth IRAs.

In other cases, marriage may suddenly make you ineligible to contribute to a Roth IRA. You may find that both you and your partner, as an unmarried couple, are both near the upper income limit for single taxpayers and are able to contribute to Roth IRAs; however, if you were to marry and combine your salaries, you may find yourselves above the Roth IRA limits. Consider a different situation for Anne and Susan. In this case, Anne and Susan each earn $100,000 in 2014. As an unmarried couple, they are each eligible to contribute fully to a Roth IRA, because they are each below the $114,000 limit. If they marry, their combined income would be $200,000, putting them above the $191,000 phase-out limit and preventing both of them from making any Roth IRA contributions at all.

Here are the income limitations:

Traditional IRA - If you are NOT covered by a retirement plan at work		
If your Filing Status is:	And Your Modified AGI is:	Then You Can Take . . .
Single or Head of Household	any amount	a full deduction up to $5,500 or $6,500 if 50 or older
Married filing jointly with a spouse who is not covered by a plan at work	any amount	a full deduction up to $5,500 or $6,500 if 50 or older
Married filing jointly with a spouse who is covered by a plan at work	$181,000 or less	a full deduction up to $5,500 or $6,500 if 50 or older
Married filing jointly with a spouse who is covered by a plan at work	more than $181,000 but less than $191,000	a partial deduction
Married filing jointly with a spouse who is covered by a plan at work	$191,000 or more	no deduction

Traditional IRA - If you ARE covered by a retirement plan at work		
If your Filing Status is:	And Your Modified AGI is:	Then You Can Take . . .
Single or Head of Household	$59,000 or less	a full deduction up to $5,500 or $6,500 if 50 or older
Single or Head of Household	more than $59,000 but less than $69,000	a partial deduction
Single or Head of Household	$69,000 or more	no deduction
Married filing jointly	$95,000 or less	a full deduction up to $5,500 or $6,500 if 50 or older
Married filing jointly	more than $95,000 but less than $115,000	a partial deduction
Married filing jointly	$115,000 or more	no deduction

Roth IRA Allowable Contributions		
If your Filing Status is:	And Your Modified AGI is:	Then You Can Take . . .
Single or Head of Household	$114,000 or less	a full deduction up to $5,500 or $6,500 if 50 or older
Single or Head of Household	more than $114,000 but less than $129,000	a partial deduction
Single or Head of Household	$129,000 or more	no deduction
Married filing jointly	$181,000 or less	a full deduction up to $5,500 or $6,500 if 50 or older
Married filing jointly	more than $181,000 but less than $191,000	a partial deduction
Married filing jointly	$191,000 or more	no deduction

Note 1: The deduction limits are accurate for 2014 and may be increased in future years.

Note 2: Your contributions can never exceed your Modified AGI

Source: www.irs.gov

Finally, if your income exceeds the limitations for a Roth IRA, consider

contributing to a nondeductible IRA. You can convert the nondeductible

IRA to a Roth IRA the minute after you make the nondeductible IRA contribution. That is exactly what I do personally, in addition to my 401(k) contribution. So, in January, 2014 I made my 2013 and 2014 nondeductible IRA contributions for me and my wife Cindy (even though she doesn't work outside the home). We immediately made Roth IRA conversions of the nondeductible IRAs. So, we put away a quick $26,000 tax-free into Roth IRAs ($6,500 each for 2013 and 2014), not including what I contributed to my 401(k). Please note this conversion of nondeductible IRA to a Roth without incurring taxable income only works if you don't have any traditional IRAs. In effect, after the monkey business, it is just like making a Roth IRA contribution, but you have to do the monkey business first to get around the limitation.

Because retirement plans allow your money to grow tax-deferred or tax-free, and we have already seen the enormous power of retirement plans, you may want to consider the impact that marriage will have on your ability to contribute to an IRA or a Roth IRA.

How Should You Plan for Your IRA and Retirement Plan After Your Death?

This is the part I really wanted to get to because this is where getting married vs. remaining unmarried makes an enormous difference.

I want your family and heirs to preserve the IRA and retirement plan for as long as possible after you die, employing the same concept as in the accumulation stage and the distribution stage, i.e., your spouse and/or your children should pay taxes later, even after you are gone. This is the third leg of my "pay taxes later" mantra. Again, assuming the family can afford it, I want them to withdraw only what they are required to withdraw from their inherited IRAs or retirement plans.

There are exceptions for Roth IRAs and Roth IRA conversions, but I will not go through that analysis here. Readers interested in Roth IRA contributions, Roth 401(k)s and Roth IRA conversions should read another one of my books, *The Roth Revolution, Pay Taxes Once and Never Again* (Morgan James, 2010).

Fundamentally, what I wanted to convey from this background section is that my "pay taxes later" premise is sound and you can rely on this concept and this advice.

The Tax Law for IRAs and Retirement Accounts as It Relates to Same-Sex Couples

The section below gets somewhat technical. But, before we get lost in a blaze of numbers and slightly difficult concepts, let's look at the big picture. There are significant opportunities for continued tax-deferral, or paying-taxes-later, for a married person who leaves his or her IRA or retirement plan to his or her surviving spouse. On the other hand, if you leave your IRA to your unmarried partner, the current law offers significantly less favorable opportunities for tax-deferral on an *Inherited IRA*. (An *Inherited IRA* is a unique asset for a non-spouse beneficiary—it is much different from an IRA that one spouse *inherits* from the other spouse.) As unfair as it is right now for unmarried partners, anticipated changes to the tax laws regarding *Inherited IRAs* for unmarried individuals are expected to make tax acceleration on *Inherited IRAs* much worse. There will be loads more to pay in taxes if you are not married. (I have written at length about the *stretch IRA*—a way for non-spouse beneficiaries to defer income taxes on *Inherited IRAs*, but that is likely to be a disappearing tactic as a result of this anticipated change to the law.)

As of 2013, married same-sex couples are entitled to inherit their deceased spouse's IRAs or retirement plans and receive the benefits of that transaction. That means, if you are legally married and your spouse dies, you can treat his or her IRA as your own by rolling it into your IRA, or by designating yourself as the account owner. This is the same favorable tax treatment that straight couples have always enjoyed. If you are not legally married, then the likely prospect (after the anticipated change to the law) is a massive income tax acceleration on the *Inherited IRA* within five years of the death of your partner. (Please note: I am assuming that the *stretch IRA,* where the non-spouse beneficiary of an IRA can continue to defer taxes for their lifetime, will be overturned in the next several years.) As shown in the analysis in the charts at the end of the chapter, if you *don't* plan appropriately, the differences between what your partner vs. your spouse could end up with could easily be measured in hundreds of thousands of dollars. Therefore, for financial reasons, if you are in a committed relationship, you hold a large IRA, and you are concerned about protecting your partner, consider getting married. And, thanks to the recent revenue ruling, it doesn't matter what state you live in as long as you get married in a state that recognizes same-sex marriage.

If you don't feel like grinding through the nitty-gritty analysis that follows this paragraph and you just want a quick view of the differences between getting married and implementing our advice vs. not getting married (which in the eyes of the IRS is: remaining "single"), please skip to the end of the chapter and look at all the graphs.

Down to the Nitty Gritty

Prior to 2013, if the owner of an IRA or retirement plan died, the IRS treated their same-sex spouse beneficiary the same way they treated a non-spouse beneficiary, which, in short, is not nearly as favorable as the treatment for a spousal beneficiary. Now, when married IRA owners leave their IRAs to their spouses, the surviving spouses derive the same favorable result whether the couple is a same-sex couple or a straight couple. So, it is important to understand the difference between the way the IRS currently treats spousal beneficiaries and non-spousal beneficiaries, but perhaps it is more important to understand how the IRS will *likely* treat non-spousal beneficiaries in the future.

Who Can Inherit an IRA?

The individual beneficiaries for IRAs (both Roth and Traditional) can be divided into two basic categories:

- Spouse beneficiary

- Non-spouse beneficiary

First, it must be understood that the IRS does not permit you to leave money in tax-deferred retirement plans indefinitely—eventually, the money must be withdrawn from the plans. These mandatory withdrawals are called Required Minimum Distributions (RMD) or sometimes Minimum Required Distributions (MRD). Below is a summary of the rules for IRAs and Roth IRAs for the owner and the two different types of beneficiaries.

- Roth IRAs

    o Roth IRA Owner - no required minimum distribution for you.

    o Spousal Beneficiary - no required minimum distribution for your spouse.

    o Non-spouse Beneficiary - must take tax-free required minimum distributions beginning the year after the Roth IRA owner died.

- IRAs

    o IRA Owner - must begin to take minimum required distributions from their IRA in the year they turn age 70. (Technically, April 1 the year following the year you turn 70½, hereafter—for simplicity—70.)

- o Spouse Beneficiary – a spouse who inherits an IRA can roll their spouse's IRA into his or her own IRA and delay RMDs until they turn age 70.

- o Non-spouse Beneficiary (under current laws) – Must take minimum required distributions starting the year after the year of death of the original IRA owner.

If an unmarried person leaves his/her IRA to his/her partner (or anyone who is not his or her spouse for that matter), the beneficiary receives a *new type of asset* called an *Inherited IRA*—this is different from inheriting an IRA from your spouse.[3] Below are the key differences between an *Inherited IRA* and a *Spousal IRA:*

- Spousal IRA

  - o RMD start date – begin taking required minimum distributions after you turn 70.

---

[3] In the past, when a same-sex partner (whether in a state-sanctioned marriage or not) was the beneficiary of an IRA he/she was treated as a non-spouse beneficiary. With the DOMA ruling and the subsequent revenue ruling, same-sex spouses (from state-sanctioned marriages) can now enjoy the benefits of Spousal IRAs.

- ○ Life expectancy used for calculating RMD – Uniform Lifetime Table is used which yields a longer life expectancy and a lower RMD.

- Inherited IRA (under current laws)

  - ○ RMD start date – begin taking required minimum distributions right away (by December 31 of the year after the owner's death), regardless of your age.

  - ○ Life expectancy used for calculating RMD - Single Life Expectancy Table is used which yields a shorter life expectancy and a higher RMD, meaning significant income tax acceleration.

For an *Inherited IRA,* under the current laws, both the RMD start date and the life expectancy values combine to force you to accelerate your income taxes and deplete your *Inherited IRA* more quickly than with a *Spousal IRA.* As a result, with an *Inherited IRA,* less and less of your money grows tax-deferred, producing less money for you overall.

A non-spouse beneficiary of an IRA *cannot* roll an *Inherited IRA* into his or her own IRA. However, (under the current laws) the owner of an *Inherited IRA* still has some ability to defer the income tax on the account. The non-spousal beneficiary, assuming he does it right and wants to "pay taxes later" should only withdraw the RMD from the *Inherited IRA*. The distribution is calculated by dividing the amount of the *Inherited IRA* by a factor that represents the life expectancy of the beneficiary.[4]

A Case Study of a Same-Sex Couple, Reviewing Finances for Surviving Spouse if One Person Dies and Leaves His IRA to His Partner/Spouse

Doctor Dan and Baker Bob are in a committed relationship. For this scenario, Doctor Dan is 78 and Baker Bob is 72. Their incomes are quite different, with Doctor Dan providing the majority of financial support for the couple's needs. Right now, they are not married, and they live in Pennsylvania. They could easily get married in New York (one of the 17 states currently recognizing same-sex marriage) and return to live in Pennsylvania, but they haven't seen a clear reason why they should, since Pennsylvania does not recognize same-sex marriages yet. In this chapter we will look at options for Doctor Dan's significant IRA.

Table 1 shows Doctor Dan's projected RMDs until his IRA is fully depleted.

---

[4] The RMD is based on the beneficiary's life expectancy as of December 31st of the year following the year the IRA
owner died. The life expectancy for different ages can be found in IRS publication 590.

This table shows how long an IRA can be extended by the owner of the IRA if he or she limits withdrawals to his RMD's even though he will obviously not live to 116.

Table 1

	Doctor Dan's Projected Distributions from His IRA (Based on the IRS Table III-Uniform Lifetime)				
Year End Dec 31	Doctor Dan's Age	IRA Balance Beg of Yr ROR 6%		Life Expectancy	Required Minimum Distribution (Taxable)
2013	78	$	992,277	20.3	$ 48,881
2014	79	$	1,000,000	19.5	$ 51,282
2015	80	$	1,005,641	18.7	$ 53,778
2016	81	$	1,008,975	17.9	$ 56,367
2017	82	$	1,009,765	17.1	$ 59,051
2047	112	$	35,178	2.6	$ 13,530
2048	113	$	22,947	2.4	$ 9,561
2049	114	$	14,189	2.1	$ 6,757
2050	115	$	7,878	1.9	$ 4,146
2051	116	$	-	0.0	$ -
		Total Distributions			$ 2,177,077

Note: No consideration for inflation has been included in this table

But, for our example, Doctor Dan dies at age 78, right after taking his distribution for that year! The balance in Doctor Dan's IRA is $1,000,000.

Baker Bob, age 72, is his beneficiary. What are the different outcomes for that money based on whether or not Doctor Dan and Baker Bob get married or remain unmarried?

The Couple Remains Unmarried (Given Current Laws on Inherited IRAs)

As part of an unmarried couple when Doctor Dan dies, Baker Bob is now the owner of an *Inherited IRA*, and Baker Bob must use the Single Life Table (from IRS publication 590) to calculate his RMDs. Baker Bob's first distribution has to be withdrawn by December 31 of the year following Doctor Dan's death, and Baker Bob's life expectancy is calculated based on how old he will be at the time the withdrawal has to be completed. That means that Baker Bob will be 73 when he has to make his first withdrawal, and his life expectancy is 14.8 years—the life expectancy of a 73-year old using the IRS Single Life Table. (Note: this life expectancy table is much less favorable than the table Baker Bob would be able to use had they been married.) The RMD for the *Inherited IRA* is calculated by dividing the balance in the account as of December 31 of the year of death, by the life expectancy of the beneficiary. Assuming that the balance of the *Inherited IRA* was $1 million, Baker Bob's first RMD would be $1 million divided by 14.8, or $67,568—which is fully taxable.[5] This technique of limiting

_____

[5] As they live in Pennsylvania, there is also the issue of inheritance taxes, but for our

distributions from *Inherited IRAs* to the RMD is referred to as the *stretch IRA*. You stretch out distributions for as long as you can based on your life expectancy to minimize the tax acceleration on the money taken out of the account—which is the same as deferring taxes as long as possible. Let's look at Table 2 to see what happens to the IRA if Doctor Dan and Baker Bob remain unmarried. The total distributions amount to $1,542,429 and the *Inherited IRA* is depleted when Baker Bob is 88 years old.

The Couple Marries

Now, let's look at what would happen if Doctor Dan and Baker Bob marry. Now that the IRS recognizes same-sex marriages, Baker Bob has two options:

1. Treat the IRA as an *Inherited IRA*. (Wrong choice—distributions according to Table 2)

2. Treat the IRA as his own IRA, by doing one of the following (Table 3)

   o A Trustee-to-trustee transfer to his own existing or new IRA

purposes we are assuming
these taxes were paid with money from outside the IRA (which is what we recommend).

○ A Spousal IRA rollover to his own existing or new

   IRA

○ Retitling Doctor Dan's IRA (the name on the account

   can just be changed, if you do not transfer the account

   to a new financial institution)

Table 2

RMDs for Unmarried Baker Bob's Inherited IRA from Dr. Dan				
Year End Dec 31	Baker Bob's Age	IRA Balance Beg of Yr ROR 6%	Life Expectancy	Required Minimum Distribution (Taxable)
2014	73	$1,000,000	14.8	$67,568
2015	74	$988,378	13.8	$71,622
2016	75	$971,762	12.8	$75,919
2017	76	$949,594	11.8	$80,474
2018	77	$921,267	10.8	$85,303
2019	78	$886,122	9.8	$90,421
2020	79	$843,444	8.8	$95,846
2021	80	$792,454	7.8	$101,597
2022	81	$732,309	6.8	$107,692
2023	82	$662,093	5.8	$114,154
2024	83	$580,815	4.8	$121,003
2025	84	$487,401	3.8	$128,263
2026	85	$380,686	2.8	$135,959
2027	86	$259,410	1.8	$144,117
2028	87	$122,211	0.8	$122,211
2029	88	$0		$0
			Total Distributions	$1,542,149

Note: No consideration for inflation has been included in this table

Table 3 reflects Baker Bob RMDs if he elects to roll Doctor Dan's IRA into his own IRA as a widowed spouse.[6][7] Instead of using the Single Life Expectancy Table that Baker Bob would have had to use had he been unmarried, Bob can now use the more favorable Uniform Lifetime Table to calculate his life expectancy. This table yields a life expectancy of 24.7 years in place of the 14.8 years that unmarried Baker Bob had to use. This longer life expectancy will result in a smaller RMD and less taxes every year. That means more money can continue to stay invested in the tax deferred IRA.. And over the course of his life expectancy, married Baker Bob winds up with $1 million dollars more in total distributions than unmarried Bob, from the same IRA account. To be fair, we didn't include the time value of money, or inflation, or the reinvested money if Baker Bob has a higher minimum required distribution of the *Inherited IRA* than his spending needs. So, the value to Baker Bob is somewhat less than $1M, but it is a lot - sufficient for Doctor Dan and Baker Bob to consider getting married.

Not only does married Baker Bob have more money than unmarried Baker Bob, married Baker Bob's financial picture even outshines Doctor Dan's.

---

[6] All versions of "Treat the IRA as his own IRA" in option 2 above would effectively yield the same result.

[7] To simplify matters, we once again assume that Baker Bob has enough after tax assets to cover the 15% non-marital Pennsylvania Inheritance Tax that he would be required to pay in 2014.

Not only is the RMD smaller for married Bob than it is for unmarried Bob, but it is even smaller than it would have been for Baker Bob's husband Doctor Dan. Because Baker Bob is younger than the doctor, his life expectancy factor is greater than Doctor Dan's: 24.7 years v 20.3 years. The longer life expectancy provides additional time for tax-deferred growth. Using the "stretch" gives Baker Bob an extra $400,000 (as compared to Doctor Dan, had he lived on) in distributions over the lifetime of the IRA that Bob inherited and rolled into his own account.

Table 3

Year End Dec 31	Baker Bob's Age	IRA Balance Beg of Yr ROR 6%	Life Expectancy	Required Minimum Distribution (Taxable)
2014	73	$1,000,000	24.7	$40,486
2015	74	$1,017,085	23.8	$42,735
2016	75	$1,032,811	22.9	$45,101
2017	76	$1,046,973	22.0	$47,590
2018	77	$1,059,346	21.2	$49,969
2019	78	$1,069,940	20.3	$52,706
2052	111	$54,617	2.9	$18,834
2053	112	$37,931	2.6	$14,589
2054	113	$24,743	2.4	$10,309
2055	114	$15,299	2.1	$7,285
2056	115	$8,495	1.9	$4,471
2057	116	$0	0.0	$0
			Total Distributions	$2,573,350

Baker Bob – Inherited IRA from Married Spouse

Note: No consideration for inflation has been included in this table

More Bad News if the Couple Remains Unmarried (Under Proposed Laws for Inherited IRAs)

We are expecting further bad news for passing on IRAs to non-spouse beneficiaries. If Doctor Dan and Baker Bob don't get married, there is the likely potential for an even less favorable outcome for Baker Bob's *Inherited IRA*.

Unfortunately, it looks like the extended tax and wealth accumulation benefits afforded by the "life expectancy" stretch for an *Inherited IRA* may soon go the way of the dinosaur. For several years, Congress has been looking for ways to reduce the benefits of an *Inherited* "stretch" *IRA*. To bring in more revenue, Congress is looking into imposing a finite term on the tax-deferred "stretch" of an *Inherited IRA*. The finite term that is being considered is five years, and many think the change will take effect in 2015 or shortly thereafter. (For more on this topic see the "Proposed Regulation Changes" at the end of the chapter.) If this happens, an IRA beneficiary will have to withdraw the balance of the entire *Inherited IRA* by the end of the fifth year after the death of the original owner.

Table 4 assumes the proposed regulation changes will occur. This scenario spreads the distributions over all five years in an effort to minimize the income tax consequences of taking a large distribution all at once.

Table 4

Unmarried Baker Bob's *Inherited IRA* –5 Year Limited				
Year End Dec 31	Baker Bob's Age	IRA Balance Beg of Yr ROR 6%	Life Expectancy	Tax-Wise Distribution 5 Yr Stretch
2014	73	$1,000,000	1.0	$225,000
2015	74	$821,500	2.0	$225,000
2016	75	$632,290	3.0	$225,000
2017	76	$431,727	4.0	$225,000
2018	77	$219,131	5.0	$219,131
			Total Distributions	$1,119,131

Note: No consideration for inflation has been included in this table

Let's Review the Numbers

As you can see when comparing all four tables, the longer the "stretch", the more financially beneficial it will be for you and your heirs.

- Table 1 represents the amount Doctor Dan would have received had he lived beyond 2014. ($2,177,077)

- Table 2 assumes that the partners never married and Baker Bob stretched the IRA for as long as he could (under the current law). ($1,542,149)

- Table 3 represents the stretch that Baker Bob can count on if he and Doctor Dan marry, and he rolls Doctor Dan's IRA into his own IRA and continues taking distributions based on his life expectancy (from the Uniform Life Expectancy table). ($2,573,350)

- Table 4 also treats the pair as unmarried, but this time the stretch is limited to the five years as we predict future law will require. ($1,119,131)

Comparing best to worst case scenarios (Table 3 to Table 4) Baker Bob would have an additional $700,000 by age 90 simply because the couple had married prior to Doctor Dan's death. (The graphs later in this chapter will show you the growth of Baker Bob's net assets.)

The Case Study Continues for the Second Generation of Heirs, Reviewing Finances for the Child of the Surviving Partner

Okay, now let's add another variable to the scenario. Imagine that Baker Bob adopted a child born in 1970, Penniless Perry. Penniless Perry is their sole beneficiary after they both pass.

The Couple Remains Unmarried (Given Current Laws on Inherited IRAs)

Both Baker Bob and Penniless Perry were heart broken when Doctor Dan

passed away. After Doctor Dan's death, the never-married Baker Bob began

taking the required minimum distributions from the *Inherited IRA* that he

received from Doctor Dan (Table 2). Only five short years later, Penniless

Perry loses his adopted father, Baker Bob at age 77. As stated previously,

Baker Bob had named Penniless Perry, his 50-year old son, as the

beneficiary of the *Inherited IRA* (the one Baker Bob inherited from Doctor

Dan—it gets a bit complicated, but stick with me). Penniless Perry *is*

required to continue taking distributions from the *Inherited IRA* according to

the calculations based on *Baker Bob's life expectancy* – not his own life

expectancy. Distributions from a second generation *Inherited IRA* are based

on the previous beneficiary's life expectancy. This is the case when someone

inherits an *Inherited IRA*. The IRS wants their tax revenue on the *Inherited*

IRA, so they force Penniless Perry to continue taking distributions at Baker

Bob's rate, despite Penniless Perry's longer life expectancy. We know that

Baker Bob took distributions from this account for five years. According to

the *stretch IRA* schedule above (Table 2), the balance left in the *Inherited*

IRA as of December 31, 2018 is $886,122. Penniless Perry's required

minimum distribution is calculated by dividing the IRA balance of $886,122

by Baker Bob's initially projected life expectancy factor – or 9.8. This means that during the year after Baker Bob's death, Penniless Perry would be

required to withdraw $90,421 from the IRA that he inherited from Baker

Bob, who inherited it from Doctor Dan – and again, that's fully taxable. The

chart below lists Penniless Perry's annual required distributions until nothing

is left in the IRA.

Penniless Perry RMD from the Second Generation *Inherited IRA* (Assuming Baker Bob and Doctor Dan Remained Unmarried)				
Year End Dec 31	Child's Age	Inherited IRA Beg Balance ROR 6%	Life Expectancy	Required Minimum Distribution (Taxable)
2019	51	$886,122	9.8	$90,421
2020	52	$843,444	8.8	$95,846
2021	53	$792,454	7.8	$101,597
2022	54	$732,309	6.8	$107,692
2023	55	$662,093	5.8	$114,154
2024	56	$580,815	4.8	$121,003
2025	57	$487,401	3.8	$128,263
2026	58	$380,686	2.8	$135,959
2027	59	$259,410	1.8	$144,117
2028	60	$122,211	0.8	$122,211
2029	61	$0		$0
			Total Distributions	$1,161,263

Note: No consideration for inflation has been included in this table

If he only took the RMDs and nothing more, Penniless Perry would receive $1,161,263 in total distributions from his father, unmarried Baker Bob. The final payout from the *Inherited IRA* would occur in 2028. If you are keeping track, you will notice that Table 5 and Table 2 are exactly the same. That is because the current law requires Penniless Perry to treat the IRA exactly as his father had. Penniless Perry assumes the "life expectancy" of his father and must continue RMDs at the same rate as his father would have been required to, had he lived.

The Couple Marries

Now let's look at the same scenario with one critical difference. Doctor Dan and Baker Bob had married. What effect does this have on Penniless Perry's inheritance? Baker Bob is 72 years old when Doctor Dan dies and leaves him the IRA which is worth $1 million. Baker Bob wisely elects to treat the IRA as his own, and he lists Penniless Perry as the sole beneficiary. Since Baker Bob is age 72, he will be required to take RMDs from his own IRA, based on the more favorable Uniform Lifetime Table. After five years of Baker Bob taking distributions, the *Inherited IRA* has a balance of $1,059,346 (much higher than in the previous example, because Bob and Dan were married).[8] When Baker Bob dies at the end of the fifth year, Penniless Perry gets to

---

[8] Refer to Table 3 to see married Baker Bob's balance at age 77.

"stretch" the *Inherited IRA*, taking required minimum distributions *based on his (Perry's) life expectancy.*

Clearly, Penniless Perry will be much better off if his dad marries. Calculating his RMDs based on his own life expectancy allows his inheritance to continue to grow tax deferred for a much longer period of time. Compare Tables 5 and 6. If Perry did nothing but collect his RMDs from his inheritance, under current law he would receive distributions for another 24 years if his father marries, resulting in total distributions of $3,193,608 instead of $1,161,263.

Further Complications for the Child if the Couple Remains Unmarried and the "Stretch" Laws Change

If Congress changes the laws and enforces a five year distribution rule on *Inherited IRAs*, a marriage between Bob and Dan becomes even more important to Penniless Perry.[9] With the five year limit in place (not a given— currently just a threat), Penniless Perry would have to deplete the second generation *Inherited IRA* according to the five year rule, vs. the slower distribution schedule that would have allowed him to continue distributions based on his father's life expectancy—10 years. That would

---

[9] Assume, for this example, that Congress changes the law after Doctor Dan dies, but before Baker Bob dies. If the change is made before Doctor Dan dies, then Baker Bob will have depleted his *Inherited IRA* (see Table 4) and there would be no IRA for Perry to inherit.

reduce what he would ultimately receive by roughly $170,000 (Total

Distributions from Table 5 minus Total Distributions from Table 7).

Table 6

Penniless Perry's *Inherited IRA* Assuming Baker Bob Married Doctor Dan				
Year End Dec 31	Adult Child's Age	IRA Balance Beg of Yr ROR 6%	Life Expectancy	Required Minimum Distribution (Taxable)
2019	51	$1,069,940	33.3	$32,130
2020	52	$1,100,078	32.3	$34,058
2021	53	$1,129,981	31.3	$36,102
2022	54	$1,159,512	30.3	$38,268
2023	55	$1,188,519	29.3	$40,564
2048	80	$748,607	4.3	$174,095
2049	81	$608,983	3.3	$184,540
2050	82	$449,909	2.3	$195,613
2051	83	$269,554	1.3	$207,349
2052	84	$65,937	0.3	$65,937
2053	85	$0	0.0	$0
			Total Distributions	$3,193,608

If Dan and Bob had married, however, Bob could have stretched his

distribution schedule for a longer period, which would mean that Perry's

Inherited IRA would be greater ($1,069,940 vs. $886,122.) And, although the five-year distribution rule would still reduce his total distributions, he would still be better off by $206,585 (Total Distributions from Table 8 minus Total Distributions from Table 7).

Table 7

		Penniless Perry Second Generation Inherited IRA from Unmarried Father - 5 Year Limited		
Year End Dec 31	Adult Child's Age	IRA Balance Beg of Yr ROR 6%	Year Following Death	Tax-Wise Distribution (Taxable)
2019	51	$886,122	1	$200,000
2020	52	$727,289	2	$200,000
2021	53	$558,926	3	$200,000
2022	54	$380,462	4	$200,000
2023	55	$191,290	5	$191,290
			Total Distributions	$991,290

Note: No consideration for inflation has been included in this table

Table 8

		Penniless Perry - Second Generation Inherited IRA Married Parents - Tax-Wise 5 Year Stretch		
Year End Dec 31	Adult Child's Age	IRA Balance Beg of Yr ROR 6%	Years After Death	Tax-Wise Distribution (Taxable)
2019	51	$1,069,940	1.0	$240,000
2020	52	$879,736	2.0	$240,000
2021	53	$678,121	3.0	$240,000
2022	54	$464,408	4.0	$240,000
2023	55	$237,872	5.0	$237,872
			Total Distributions	$1,197,872

Note: No consideration for inflation has been included in this table

Let's Summarize the Numbers for the Case Study

First Let's Simply Look at the Finances for the Couple

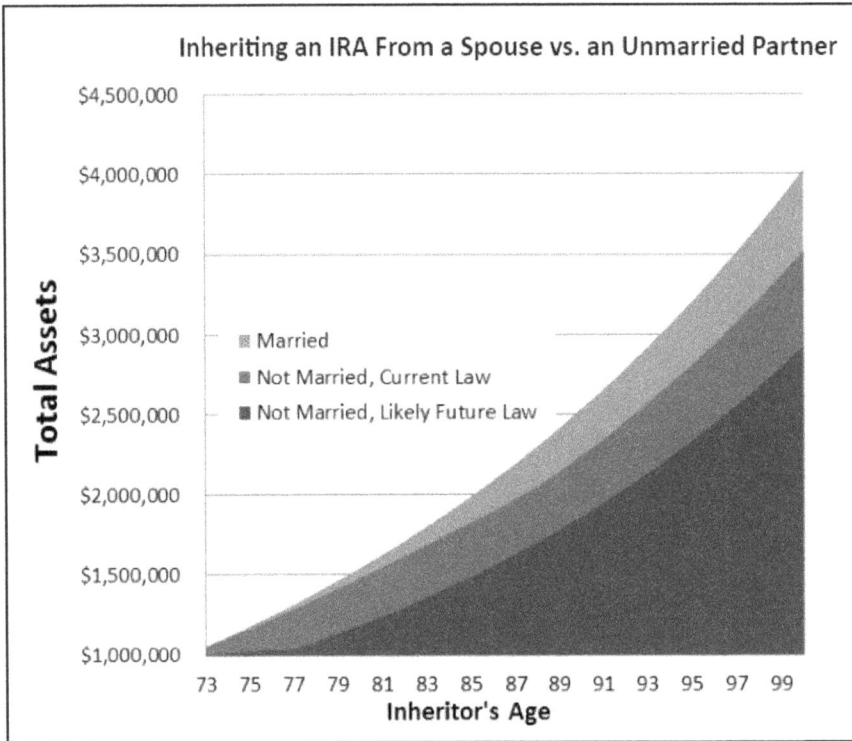

Inheriting an IRA From a Spouse vs. an Unmarried Partner

- Married
- Not Married, Current Law
- Not Married, Likely Future Law

(Total Assets axis: $1,000,000 to $4,500,000; Inheritor's Age axis: 73 to 99)

The assumptions for this graph include the following:

1. Includes 3% Rate of Inflation

2. Includes 6% Rate of Return

We compiled the data from Tables 2, 3 and 4 and added a 6% Rate of Return and a 3% Rate of Inflation to generate the graph above.[10] Had we used a

---

[10] Although the RMD varies from one example to another, we assume that the living expenses will not vary. All money withdrawn from the IRA that is not needed for living expenses is assumed to be put into an after-tax investment and grows without tax-deferral.

higher Rate of Return, the differences would be far more dramatic. We can plainly see that Baker Bob will have more assets available

for his retirement years, if he and Doctor Dan marry. Ten years from the date of his inheritance, married (and widowed) Baker Bob would have an additional $94,000 in invested assets as compared to what he would have had if he had remained unmarried and stretched his Inherited IRA. The advantage of getting married becomes even greater the longer Baker Bob lives. When we look at unmarried Baker Bob under the anticipated law change, we see at age 90, married Baker Bob will have accumulated over $380,000 more than the unmarried Baker Bob, who had to deplete the IRA within five years. This puts him into a much higher tax bracket and significantly reduces his savings.

Managing an Ira After Death Is Very Important for The Well-Being of The Next Generation

Because Baker Bob and Doctor Dan married, Baker Bob was able to roll the IRA that he inherited from Doctor Dan into his own IRA account. In turn, this allowed Baker Bob's son, Penniless Perry, to calculate his RMDs based on his own life expectancy (as opposed to Baker Bob's life expectancy for a second generation *Inherited IRA*). Penniless Perry's *Inherited IRA* now grows tax deferred for a longer period of time. The graph below includes Tables 5, 6 & 7 adjusted with a Rate of Return of 6% and an Inflation Rate of 3%. The difference in investment income from a married parent's IRA as opposed to an unmarried parent's IRA could amount to millions in additional income over Penniless Perry's lifetime.

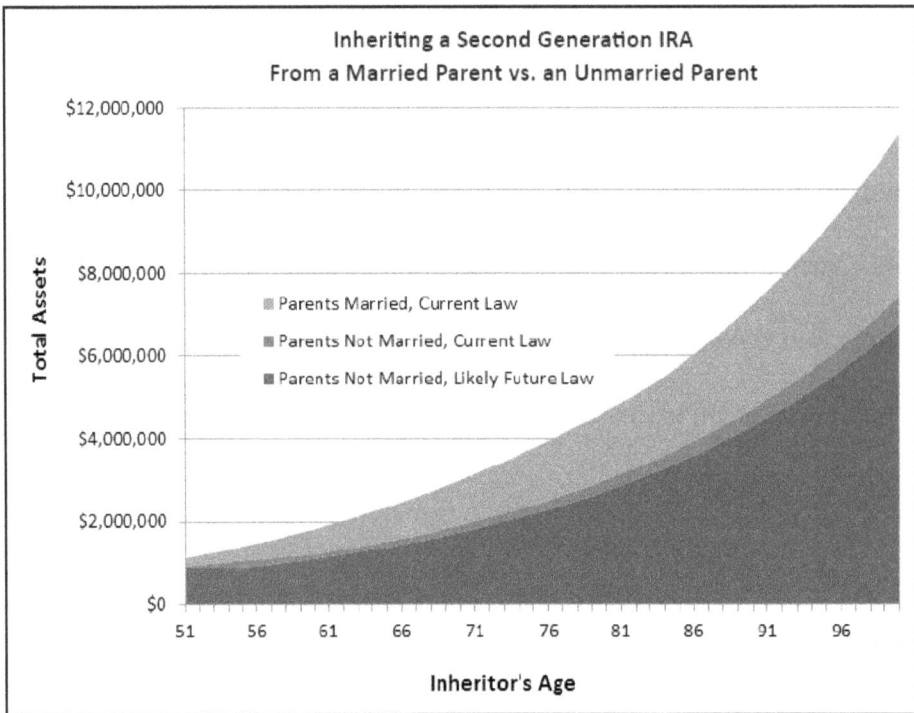

Inheriting a Second Generation IRA
From a Married Parent vs. an Unmarried Parent

- Parents Married, Current Law
- Parents Not Married, Current Law
- Parents Not Married, Likely Future Law

(Total Assets vs. Inheritor's Age)

The assumptions for this graph include the following:

1. Includes 3% Rate of Inflation

2. Includes 6% Rate of Return

Just by getting married, Baker Bob is able to leave an additional $183,000 to Penniless Perry from the IRA he inherited from Doctor Dan and rolled into his own. Penniless Perry, son of married partners, also gets the benefit of an additional 24 to 29 year stretch because he can base his RMDs on his own life (first generation *Inherited IRA*) expectancy as opposed to the life expectancy of his unmarried father (second generation *Inherited IRA*). Assuming that Penniless Perry reinvests all of his RMDs into after-tax investments, and that his father was married, he would earn additional income by age 60 of $1,830,046 v $1,113,549 if his father remained unmarried; by age 70 of $3,003,499 v $1,749,269; and age 80 of $4,682,296 v $2,747,918.

We could present this analysis in different ways using different assumptions. The conclusion will likely be the same. Same-sex couples with significant IRAs who are otherwise inclined to get married, should get married for the financial protection of the beneficiary of the IRA.

Well, you made it over the hump; you've accumulated well and planned for your retirement. What happens next? You need an estate plan for your heirs. Please picture yourself after the necessary changes have been made, knowing that you have set things up in the most beneficial manner for your family. If you marry, your spouse will be grateful with the gift of security you are providing. Imagine how good you'll feel knowing that you have to a large extent protected your estate from the IRS and got the most from your Social Security for you and your partner/spouse.

If you are already married and all of your documents are in great shape (and now after reading this book you will be in a better position to know), you should be applauded! If, however, things aren't in great shape or if you have questions, please read on and then take action so that your legacy won't be decimated by taxes.

Proposed Regulation Changes

As previously mentioned, it looks like the extended tax and wealth accumulation benefits afforded by the *stretch IRA* may soon go the way of the dinosaur. In 2012, Senate Finance Committee Chairman Max Baucus proposed limiting the *stretch IRA* to five-years-after-death for a non-spouse beneficiary, effectively making the beneficiary pay all the income taxes on the *Inherited IRA* over those five years. Thankfully, that proposal was withdrawn for lack of support. The idea reappeared, however, in April 2013 in President Obama's budget proposals, and made a grand entrance in the summer of 2013 when the measure was reintroduced as a part of a bill to reduce future student loan debt. Killing the long benefit of the *stretch IRA*, they felt, would provide the revenue necessary to reduce student loan interest rates for college students, for one year. This bill was introduced in June of 2013 and died in the Senate with a vote of 51-49 in favor of another bill to reduce student loan interest rates. To be fair, the bill would have had a tougher time getting through the House, but President Obama wanted to sign it. It is becoming increasingly clear that this measure, or a similar one, may eventually pass — some say as early as 2015. I have had numerous discussions with top IRA experts in the country and everyone seems to agree that the *stretch IRA* as we know it now will be gone in several years. On *The Lange Money Hour*, both Ed Slott, the best known IRA expert in the country, and Sy Goldberg, a politically connected IRA expert, said the stretch as we know it will not survive. (Please see www.paytaxeslater.com for the sound file and the transcript of those shows). Congress, in all its wisdom, has decided that forcing your non-spousal heirs to pay income taxes on your entire IRA or retirement plan within five years of your death will provide them (Congress) with a quick budget fix. Unfortunately, that fix will have sad consequences for your children or grandchildren. It will also have dire financial implications for same-sex couples who don't get married, where the large IRA owner predeceases the other partner.

Does this possible change in the law mean that you shouldn't bother investigating how a *stretch IRA* might benefit your estate plan? Of course not! A beneficiary who is your spouse will still retain the right to treat your IRA as his or her own – thus prolonging the "stretch" for his or her own lifetime. No one is proposing a change in how the IRA will be treated if you name your spouse as the beneficiary. However, there could be serious consequences for a partner who is your IRA beneficiary, *but not your spouse.* For this reason alone, every committed same-sex couple should consider formal marriage to protect the spouse who is likely to inherit the retirement assets. The line of demarcation will be the date of the IRA owner's death. If that individual dies before the legislation is passed, then their non-spouse beneficiary will get the stretch afforded by the Single Life Table discussed above. If the IRA owner dies after the proposed legislation is passed, their non-spouse beneficiary will have to pay tax on the entire account within five years. You can see that this legislation will have a significant impact on the finances of your non-spouse partner. If you want to receive updates on the status of these changes, please sign up for our newsletter at www.outestateplanning.com.

In the past, even if you understood the laws governing inheriting IRAs, you might not have factored them into your decision of whether or not to get married because the IRS treated your spouse or your partner as a non-spouse. Well, all that has changed. It is very important that both you and your beneficiary understand how your options change when you become a legally recognized married couple.

The biggest action point in this chapter is that if you are not currently married, you should consider getting married in a state that recognizes same-sex marriage whether you live in that state or not. For example, if you are a same-sex couple living in Pennsylvania (where same-sex marriage is not currently recognized) and one partner has a substantial IRA that he or she wants to leave to the other partner, there are huge potential tax advantages to your partner if you get married in New York (or any other state where same-sex marriage is recognized) and come back home to Pennsylvania to live.

You might think I have stressed this point so often that I must have a cousin in New York who performs same-sex couple marriages. It turns out, I do have a cousin in New York who is also an attorney, and married to another man. After I started this book, I found out he became a judge and could legally perform same-sex marriages!

3

Same-Sex Couples and Social Security Benefits

*Ultimately I think what people care about, particularly on an issue like
Social Security, is not really what's right and what's left but what's right
and what's wrong.*

John Podesta

Main Topics

• What is the current policy of the Social Security Administration regarding same-sex couples?

• Could the prospect of Social Security benefits influence our decision to legally marry?

• When should someone begin taking Social Security?

• What are some of the best strategies to maximize Social Security benefits?

Key Idea

Unless absolutely essential, delay taking Social Security as long as possible.

Living a long time and running out of money is the big concern. The longer

you live, the bigger the difference in the amount you collect and the

greater your long-term financial security.

Significant Social Security Benefits for Married Couples

This chapter is one of the two most important and potentially life-changing chapters in this book. The other is Chapter 2 on IRAs and retirement plans. Why? Because they address some of the most compelling reasons to make good financial decisions for you and your partner's long-term financial security, including the decision of whether or not to get married. The first premise to be explained in detail is that there are significant Social Security benefits for married couples, which are *not available* for two non-married partners. Up until 2013, the Social Security Administration did not recognize legal, state sanctioned same-sex marriages for the purpose of allowing Social Security benefits. Under the old law you were treated as two unmarried people—to your financial detriment.

That changed in 2013. The Social Security Administration now recognizes same-sex marriages *in states that also recognize same-sex marriages*. This has created a financial planning bonanza for legally married same-sex couples because they are potentially able to collect Social Security spousal benefits and spousal survivor benefits (to be explained later). For couples that haven't yet taken the nuptial plunge, and who live in states that recognize same-sex marriage, it could easily tip the scale toward getting married in order to enjoy enormous additional Social Security benefits.

The advice we offer here applies immediately to couples who married in, and live in, states that recognize same-sex marriage. Marriage should also be strongly considered by residents of states that do not currently recognize same-sex marriage. We believe that either Congress, the Social Security Administration, or the courts will eventually have to provide legally married residents of states that don't currently recognize same-sex marriage with equal treatment under the law —meaning they'll be given the same rights to collect Social Security as residents of states that do recognize same-sex marriage. If we are correct in our forecast, all legally married same-sex couples, regardless of where they are domiciled when they apply for Social Security benefits or where they live, will be treated as a legally married couple. It will be a huge financial benefit for same-sex married couples.

The Big Picture

Imagine two identical couples – they are the same ages, they have the same assets, and the same earnings records. One couple gets married and takes advantage of the strategies recommended in this chapter. The other couple remains unmarried and both partners start collecting Social Security at age 62. Twenty years pass, and their lifestyles and spending are identical. Eventually, the partner with the stronger earnings record of both couples dies. The financial situations of the two surviving partners is now drastically different:

the survivor of the couple who got married and followed our advice

has $400,000, the survivor of the couple that didn't get married, and

chose to take Social Security early, is nearly broke.

The details follow later in this chapter. This example isolates the difference

due to Social Security benefits. Granted, it is not likely to mirror anyone's

situation exactly, but it does highlight the point that there could be enormous

financial benefits for same-sex couples who get married and follow the

advice in this chapter.

The Social Security spousal benefit alone may provide a compelling reason

for same-sex couples to get married in a state that recognizes same-sex

marriage. If you agree with us and anticipate that the law will change, and

that Social Security spousal benefits will most likely be paid to all legally

married same-sex couples regardless of their state of residence, then there is

even stronger motivation to get married. For high-earning couples, or even

more compellingly, when there is one higher-earning partner/spouse and one

lower-earning partner/spouse, the Social Security spousal benefit could

potentially be measured in the hundreds of thousands of dollars (described

below). A significant factor to consider is that, if the higher-earning spouse is

the first to die, Social Security increases the monthly income for the lower-earning spouse following the death of the higher earning spouse. For couples of more modest means, the difference may not be as dramatic in terms of absolute numbers; nevertheless, getting married in a state that recognizes same-sex marriage *and* taking the appropriate steps can provide a solid base for both of you in retirement during your joint lifetimes, and after the death of your spouse.

Unfortunately, sophisticated Social Security strategies are unfamiliar territory for same-sex couples, advisors to same-sex couples and even most financial advisors to straight couples. Granted, few straight couples know enough about the nuances of Social Security strategies to get the most from their benefits. But I do. In this chapter, I combine that knowledge with what I know about same-sex couple laws after the recent DOMA ruling and its aftermath.

It is, however, crucial to understand that there are multiple strategies for maximizing Social Security benefits, and that the vast majority of Social Security recipients—whatever their sexual orientation or marriage status— fail to apply any of these perfectly legal strategies to maximize their benefits. My objective here is to point out the advantages of spousal benefits for legally married same-sex couples, and to recommend strategies that will help you to get the most out of your Social Security benefits.

Let me also add that decisions about whether or not it makes financial sense for you to get married, when you should collect Social Security benefits, and, to the extent that you have a choice, which Social Security benefits you should collect, should not be considered in isolation. Because of the enormous financial implications that I'm about to show you, you should keep in mind that one decision will often have a consequence in a different area. For instance, did you know that there is an advantageous synergy that comes from combining the timing of Social Security benefits and making multiple Roth IRA conversions? Assuming you fit the profile (including being married), a combination of one of the Social Security claiming strategies described later in this chapter and a series of Roth conversions starting after retirement, but possibly ending at age 70, warrants serious consideration. Above all, your personal situation, the personal situation of your partner/spouse, and your collective financial/retirement plans should all factor into your decision about how and when to claim Social Security benefits.

My objective is to point out the advantages and disadvantages of some scenarios and hopefully motivate you to get more information for your particular circumstances—either on your own or with the help of an expert financial advisor.

Chapter Overview on Social Security

This chapter includes:

- a summary of the critical features of Social Security benefits applicable to everyone who has either

    - paid into Social Security through payroll taxes and has worked long enough to have earned a benefit or

    - who is married to such a worker;

- the current policy of the Social Security Administration regarding same-sex couples; and

- strategies to maximize Social Security benefits.

This chapter also addresses:

- how the options available to married couples that affect Social Security benefits might have an impressive impact on your decision to legally marry your partner;

- how and why you both need to think about timing your
  application for Social Security benefits; and

- whether it might be advantageous to use the *"Apply and Suspend"*
  technique we introduce in this chapter.

My Big Assumption... but I Could be Wrong

Here is what the IRS said:

> The U.S. Department of the Treasury and the Internal Revenue
> Service (IRS) today ruled that same-sex couples, legally married in
> jurisdictions that recognize their marriages, will be treated as married
> for federal tax purposes. *The ruling applies regardless of whether the*
> *couple lives in a jurisdiction that recognizes same-sex marriage or a*
> *jurisdiction that does not recognize same-sex marriage* [emphasis
> mine]. August 29, 2013.

Consider the meaning of these phrases: "legally married", "married for
federal tax purposes" and "regardless of where the couple lives". So even if
you live in a state that does not recognize same-sex marriage, the IRS will
recognize your marriage if it was performed in a state that recognizes same-
sex marriage. What may be somewhat confusing, though, is that (as of this
writing) you are only considered "married" with respects to any federal tax
returns that you are filing. I might be wrong, but I feel confident that the

Social Security Administration or the courts or Congress will change their policies as they relate to Social Security to mirror that of the IRS. On the Social Security Administration's website, they indicate that they are "working with the Department of Justice to develop and implement policy and processing instructions on this issue."[11] *This issue* refers to being legally married, but living in a state that prohibits or does not recognize same-sex marriages.

The section below explains the *current policy* (as of March 2014) of the Social Security Administration regarding same-sex couples. As will be seen, there will be enormous advantages for same-sex couples living in states that do not currently recognize same-sex marriages, to get married in a state that does recognize same-sex marriage *and* to take appropriate action well before the Social Security Administration's policy mirrors the IRS policy. Even the Social Security Administration is saying "we encourage you to apply right away, even if you aren't sure you are eligible. Applying now will preserve your filing date, which we use to determine the start of potential benefits." For legally married residents of the states that currently recognize same-sex marriages, including New York, California, and Massachusetts just to

---

[11] https://faq.ssa.gov/link/portal/34011/34019/Article/3547/Do-I-qualify-for-benefits-if-I-live-in-a-place-that-prohibits-or-does-not-recognize-same-sex-marriages-or-other-legal-same-sex-relationships

mention a few, the strategies described below are compelling and you don't have to wait for any changes in the law or current policy to realize their advantages. That said, no matter where you live or your legal status as a couple, *don't apply for Social Security without thinking through your best strategy*; you could do more harm than good. Take the Social Security Administration's message, "we encourage you to apply right away, even if you aren't sure you are eligible" as a statement of *potential eligibility*, not necessarily your best long-term financial strategy.

If you can't stand going through the details of the rest of this chapter, please skip to the end and read the recommended action points. Please at least glance at the graph "Social Security Single vs. Married with "*Apply and Suspend*" at the end of the chapter.

The Basics

I'm going to begin by explaining the basics of Social Security benefits—and for now, we will forget about the marriage issue. A point of contention regarding Social Security is when to begin receiving benefits: as soon as you are eligible, several years later, or even waiting until you are age 70. Let's just talk about whether it makes sense, in general, to take Social Security early. For discussion's sake, let's assume your attitude is, "Well, gee, I'm retired, I'm 62 years old, I've been paying into this system for my whole life, and now it's time for me to get some money out." So you sign up and start receiving benefits. Should you have waited?

Comparison of Taking Social Security at Age 62 or Age 70

First, it is important to understand that the dollar amount of your retirement benefit depends upon the age at which you begin to collect it. Let's assume you were born between 1943 and 1954. Your full retirement age (FRA) is 66. This is set by law. The amount you will get if you begin to collect benefits at age 66 is called your Primary Insurance Amount (PIA). If you begin to collect benefits at a different age, the amount you will receive is a function of your PIA. If you begin early, you obviously start receiving an income earlier, but allowing for interest, etc. (details to follow), you will receive less per month than if you had waited. If you start taking benefits at 62, the earliest age at which you can begin to collect benefits, you will suffer the maximum reduction in benefits. If you begin to collect benefits after full retirement age, you will receive larger benefits. You can get the largest benefit by waiting until age 70. So, the two extremes would be signing up for benefits at age 62, or waiting and taking them at age 70. The earlier you collect, the lower your benefit will be for the rest of your life.

The following table shows the percentage of your PIA (the amount you would get at age 66) that you will receive if you begin to collect benefits early.

Apply at age	Benefit will be % of PIA If FRA = 66
62	75.0%
63	80.0%
64	86.7%
65	93.3%
66	100%

For every year that you wait to collect benefits after full retirement age (FRA) you will earn an extra 8% per year. Please note neither of these charts includes cost of living adjustments (COLA), which in both cases make the advantages of waiting even greater.

Apply at age	Benefit will be % of PIA If FRA = 66
66	100%
67	108%
68	116%
69	124%
70	132%

Running the Numbers for a Single Social Security Recipient

To accurately compare the financial benefits of waiting until age 70 to take

benefits, vs. starting to take them at age 62, we are going to assume that you

will not spend any of your benefits from the time you start collecting until

the time you reach age 70. In fact, we are going to assume that you will

reinvest all the benefits you've received, until age 70. If we don't make that

assumption, it is extremely difficult to make an "apples to apples"

comparison. For our example, we have two single people with identical

earnings records. One starts collecting at age 62 and invests all the benefits at

4%. The other one waits until age 70 to begin collecting. The red line on the

chart below represents the accumulation over time for the 62-year-old, and

the blue line represents the accumulation over time for the one who waited

until age 70 to begin taking benefits. If you take benefits at 62, you receive

75% of what you would have received if you waited until age 66, and if you

wait until age 70 you will receive 132% of what you would have received

had you taken benefits at age 66. By waiting until age 70 you will see a 76%

increase in your monthly benefit from what you would have received at age

62. (The math here may not be immediately obvious so, consider an

example. If your PIA at 66 is $100, and you decide to begin benefits at age

62 you will get $75. If you wait until 70, you will get $132. The additional

amount you would get for waiting is $57 [$132-$75 = $57]. The percentage by which you will have increased your benefit is 76% [$57/$75].)

The person who waits until age 70 to take Social Security and lives past age 81 will ultimately receive a lot more in benefits than the person who takes the benefit at age 62 (age 81 is roughly the breakeven point). That assumes a 4% (after tax) rate of return. If you assume a lower rate of return, the breakeven age would be even younger. Now, you might think that age 81 is a long time to wait to breakeven, but let's think about the issues of long-term financial goals and concerns in more detail.

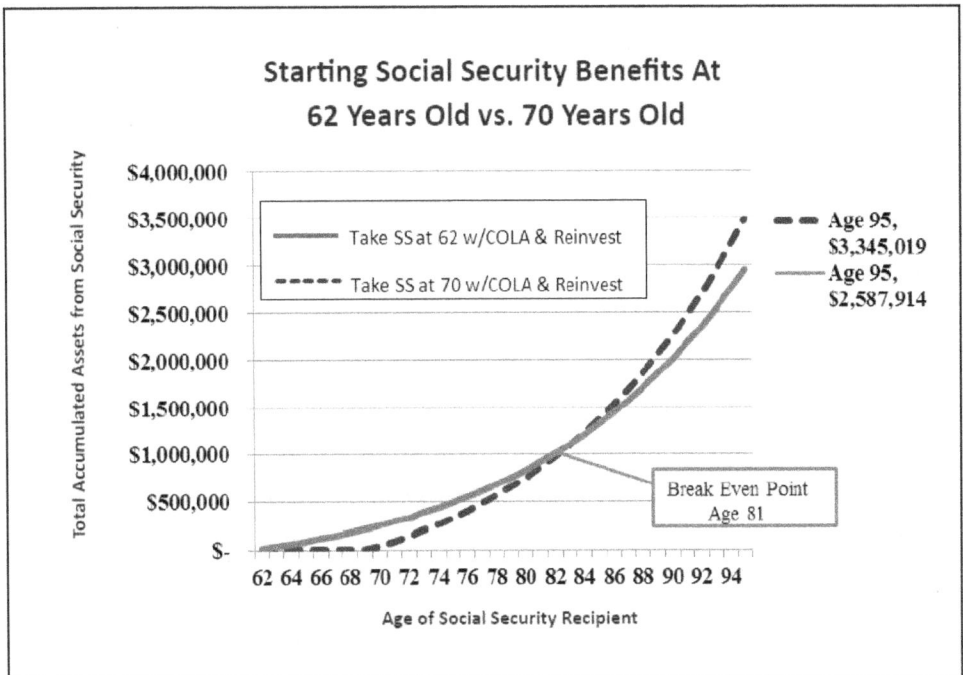

If you don't absolutely need your Social Security benefits to maintain a reasonable lifestyle, and you anticipate living past age 81 (or even if you think you only have a reasonable chance of surviving until age 81), here is why you should consider waiting. You may think the conservative thing to do is to take it early because if you don't survive to age 81 you will "win." That is the way I used to think about it until I was enlightened.

Larry Kotlikoff, an economist at Boston University, and a guest on *The Lange Money Hour*, taught me a better way to think about it.[12] "Don't think like an actuary," declares Larry, "think like an economist." You have to think about what you *should be* afraid of and what you *should not* be afraid of for financial purposes. For financial purposes, you should not fear an early death. You will be dead, and therefore you will have no more financial problems. What you should be afraid of, though, is living a long time and not having enough income to meet your needs. The big problem you could face is not having enough money to comfortably sustain you over your *extended* lifetime. What you are doing when you hold off on taking Social Security is ensuring a greater income into your old age. In our example, if you live to age 95, the difference, in terms of the total amount collected, would be $3,345,019 vs. $2,587,914. That's more than $750,000 additional dollars in your own pocket. The key concept to understand is this: the longer you live,

---

[12] I have a radio show, The Lange Money Hour, and I talk with the top experts in the areas of retirement and estate planning and investments. Larry was a guest on the show when he enlightened me. There are115 hours of archived shows, including transcripts, which are available at www.paytaxeslater.com.

the bigger the difference in the amount you collect and the greater your financial security if you live a long time. Let's face it, if you begin taking benefits at age 62 and you don't absolutely need them, and you die shortly thereafter…well you are dead. No more worries. "But wait," you say, "what about my spouse who is still alive. I want to take care of him/her too." Exactly. Remember, in the example above we are only talking about an individual who is *not* married. As will be seen, marriage introduces a completely new set of concerns that make waiting longer to collect benefits even more lucrative. Yes, there is certainly a chance that the Social Security Administration will change its policy in a way that is disadvantageous to you. However, every knowledgeable person I have spoken to about this issue, including Larry Kotlikoff, who is pretty tuned-in politically, says that the risks of taking Social Security benefits early far outweigh the risks of significant reductions for people who are currently age 62 or older.

You should rest assured. You are going to get Social Security benefits as long as you are alive…   **Bill Bradley**

Delay Claiming Benefits to Provide Long-Term Security for Your Surviving Spouse

Although spousal benefits will be discussed in greater detail later in the chapter, one critical point that needs to be understood immediately is that, typically, the surviving spouse is going to receive benefits based on the higher of the two earnings records. So, by holding off until age 66 or 70, as opposed to collecting at age 62, you are not only creating a higher benefit for the rest of your life, but you're also protecting your lower-earning surviving spouse in the event you predecease him or her. This is an extremely important area, and may even be seen by some as so critical for protecting the lower-earning spouse, that this fact alone may justify getting married. If the objective is to have enough money to live comfortably for the rest of both of your lives, then the person with the stronger earnings record will usually be well advised to wait to collect.

Scenario 1: Married, Surviving Spouse Collects Survivor Benefit

Let's assume that the spouse with the stronger earnings record waits until age 70 to collect benefits, and her benefit grows to $3,000/month. Let's assume her lower earning spouse has a benefit on her own lower earnings record of $2,000/month. The spouse with the stronger earnings record then dies. The surviving spouse, even though her benefit is only $2,000/month, can claim

the full amount (which would be the $3,000/month), provided that the

surviving spouse has reached full retirement age of 66. Calculating the

survivor benefit can be more complicated if the survivor hasn't reached full

retirement age, or if the deceased spouse claimed benefits before full

retirement age.

Scenario 2: Unmarried, No Survivor Benefit for Surviving Partner

The couple in question is not married. Let's assume the same benefits: the

lower-earner's benefit is $2,000/month and the higher-earning partner's is

$3,000/month. Then the higher-earning partner dies. The surviving partner

will continue to receive $2,000 /month. The other partner's benefits stop

when he or she dies. No survivor benefit is paid to the surviving unmarried

partner.

The potential for the lower earner to take a survivor benefit if the stronger

earner dies first could mean the difference between being broke and being

marginally okay, assuming that there are no other resources. This is

especially true if there is a big difference between the higher earner's benefit

and the lower earner's benefit. The issue of providing for the partner with the

lower earnings record is critical. Providing for the lower-earning spouse, in my opinion, should weigh heavily in the decision of when the spouse with

the stronger earnings record should begin collecting Social Security benefits.

It is not just an individual issue—it is a family issue. I am not alone in

endorsing the general concept of the higher-earning spouse holding off on

collecting Social Security. I am only applying a well-documented (but not

generally known) concept from the straight couple world to the same-sex

couple world. Four guests from *The Lange Money Hour*, all experts in their

respective fields, have all basically said that the spouse with the stronger

earning record should wait at least until age 66, but probably until age 70, to

start collecting Social Security, not just to protect themselves, but perhaps

more importantly, to protect the surviving spouse.[13] The four experts who are

in agreement on this concept are:

Jane Bryant Quinn, one of the top financial writers in the country

Mary Beth Franklin, former editor of *Kiplinger's Personal Finance Magazine*

Larry Kotlikoff, economist, Boston University

---

[13] Again, all these shows are archived, with a transcript, and are available at www.paytaxeslater.com.

Kathleen Sindell, author, *Social Security: Maximize Your Benefits*

All the experts and authors mentioned above (including me) hate when the spouse with the stronger earnings record begins to collect at age 62. Waiting to start collecting Social Security is probably even more important for women (who generally have longer life expectancies) and for couples whose income after retirement is mostly or entirely made up of Social Security benefits.

Coming Out Later in Life and Protecting Your Partner

When Sue, a lesbian, was young, she began a traditional life, married a man and had children.

She came out after her husband died, and now has a female partner. She is very connected to her children and grandchildren. Though she wants to provide for her partner, she feels compelled to leave her children and grandchildren all of her money, much of which came from her deceased husband's retirement plan. With her estate attorney, she drafts wills, trusts, IRA beneficiary designations, etc., leaving everything to a combination of her children and grandchildren. Taking my advice, she waited until 70 to begin collecting Social Security benefits on her own earnings record and now has a benefit of $3,000/month. Her new partner has a benefit of $1,000/month, is retired and can't go back to work, and has no other financial resources.

If Sue does nothing and dies, her partner will continue to get $1,000/month and, unless something unexpected happens, will spend the rest of her life in dire poverty. If Sue marries her partner (and they sign an effective pre-nuptial agreement), Sue can still leave her children and grandchildren all her money. The difference is that her spouse (formerly her partner) would become eligible to collect a spousal benefit (spousal benefits will be explained later in this chapter) during their joint lives ($1,500 if she is full retirement age), and a survivor benefit at Sue's death ($3,000 if she is full retirement age). $3,000/month is a lot better than $1,000/month. The great thing here is that the increase didn't cost Sue, or Sue's children or grandchildren, one nickel.

There are also some stunning strategies where multiple divorced and current spouses can collect on the same high-earner's record, but that is beyond the scope of this book. Nevertheless, if you are divorced you may be eligible for Social Security benefits based on your ex-spouse's earnings record. You should pursue this with the appropriate expert. In the words of one divorced client who "got rid of her husband" then found out she could collect on his Social Security earnings record: "Finally, the no good S.O.B. is good for something!"

The Current Policy of the Social Security Administration

Now, this is where distinctions between straight marriages and same-sex marriages get a bit more complicated. For straight marriages, it doesn't matter where you got married because all of those marriages are recognized by both the state and the federal government. Currently, however, the Social Security Administration uses the laws and policies of the *state of residence* to determine if an individual is "legally married," meaning able to receive spousal Social Security benefits. To be entitled to spousal or survivor benefits, applicants must marry in a state permitting same-sex marriage, *and* be domiciled at the time of application for Social Security in a state that permits same-sex marriage, or have moved to a state that permits same-sex marriage while the claim is pending final determination.

(To see the current policy, go to http://www.ssa.gov/same-sexcouples.)

But don't let that policy stop you from getting married in a state that recognizes same-sex marriages, if you are living in one of the 33 states that do not recognize same-sex marriage. Social Security applications from residents of states that do not recognize same-sex marriages *will be put on hold* until new instructions are issued. So, if you believe you could be entitled to spousal or survivor benefits (and that applying for them immediately is your best Social Security strategy), it is imperative that you apply as soon as possible in order to preserve your filing date. Your filing date will determine your potential starting date for any Social Security benefits to which you are found to be eligible.

As a final twist, it may be prudent to apply for Social Security benefits even if you are not legally married, but you are in a civil union or domestic partnership in a state that recognizes such a union or partnership. (Again, only if applying for benefits *immediately* is your best Social Security strategy).

Strategies to Maximize Social Security Benefits

I will begin by telling you the one resource that you *should not* use to identify the best benefits strategy for you. Do not use the person who works for the Social Security Administration as your Social Security expert. That person is not likely a long-term strategic thinker. He or she is hopefully capable when it comes to providing you with information about your earnings record and your estimated benefit amounts, and for processing your application. Unfortunately, his or her expertise is unlikely to extend to Social Security planning, and most likely won't extend to planning for your overall financial well-being in retirement. I want to scream when I hear, "Oh, I know you told me to hold off on collecting Social Security but the person at the Social Security office said I should start collecting at 62. That's like taking the advice of the teller at the bank who says you should buy an annuity, instead of taking the advice of the CPA/Attorney with 30 years of experience who says you are you better off investing in a portfolio of well-diversified index funds. The person who works for Social Security is not likely to be the person you want to use for strategic decision making. To be fair, there are some smart, capable people who work for the Social Security Administration, who may be able to give you sophisticated retirement and estate planning advice regarding your Social Security options, but I would not count on that person being the one who processes your application.

The goal for most married couples (whether same-sex or opposite-sex) is to identify and, if appropriate, collect the maximum Social Security benefits available for their lifetimes and, ultimately, the remaining lifetime of the surviving spouse. Because spousal and survivor benefits are only available to married couples, any strategy in which spousal and/or survivor benefits are collected will result in cumulative benefits that exceed those available to single people. A strategy such as the *"Apply and Suspend"* strategy discussed below is only available to certain married couples. It maximizes both survivor benefits *and* benefits during the couple's joint life times, and demonstrates a compelling reason for same-sex couples otherwise inclined, to strongly consider marriage.

Spousal Benefits

A spousal benefit is a Social Security benefit paid to someone based upon their spouse's earning history. You can receive Social Security based upon your own earning history, or, if your spouse has a much higher earnings record than you do, you can choose to receive a spousal benefit (50% of your spouse's PIA if it is claimed at full retirement age). The lower wage earner can often collect a higher Social Security benefit based upon their spouse's benefit. The higher wage earner's monthly benefit is not affected in any way. The lower wage earner is eligible to collect more, simply because they are married. Generally, spousal benefits are available during a couple's joint lifetimes.

Consider an example. Sue and Mary are the same age and they got married and are living in New York, a state that recognizes same-sex marriage. Sue has a $2,500/month benefit at age 66. Mary, her spouse, on her own earnings record, has a $1,000/month benefit at age 66. At age 66, Sue can collect her $2,500 benefit. Instead of the $1,000/month benefit due Mary based on her own earnings record, Mary can collect $1,250 (half of Sue's $2,500) per month as a spousal benefit.

Using the Apply and Suspend Strategy to Enhance Cumulative Benefits

My favorite Social Security strategy involves one spouse, usually the one with the stronger earnings record, *applying* for, and then *suspending* collection of his or her benefits: the stronger earning spouse applies for Social Security benefits, and then suspends benefits until age 70. What is the difference between doing Apply and Suspend at 66 and simply waiting until age 70 to collect? For the person applying and suspending, there is no difference. But, by applying and suspending, you allow your spouse to collect spousal benefits based on your earnings record. Now this is the fun part. In this situation, neither individual will be collecting benefits based on his or her own earnings records. Both individuals will continue to earn credit that will enhance their own benefits when they do begin to collect on their own records. In other words, the advantages of waiting to collect Social Security that was discussed earlier will still apply to both spouses even though one of the spouses is collecting a spousal benefit based on the other spouse's earnings record.

Here's How It Works

When the higher earner turns 66, she applies for Social Security and then immediately suspends her benefits. The lower earner can then file a restricted application for Social Security benefits (applying for spousal benefits, but not all of the Social Security benefits that this spouse is entitled to). From ages 66 to 70, the lower earner collects this spousal benefit. In the meantime, the benefits for both spouses continue to grow, just as if neither of the two had collected any Social Security benefits at all. When the lower earner reaches 70, she is then able to choose between the Social Security benefit based upon her own earnings, or she can continue to receive the spousal benefit, obviously whichever is greater. What is really fun is that even though she was collecting a spousal benefit between age 66 and 70, her own personal benefit was not reduced and actually continued to grow as if she had not claimed a nickel. At age 70, the higher earner "unsuspends" her benefits and begins collecting her Social Security. Claiming a spousal benefit does not impact the earning record or the allowable benefits for either of the spouses. So, in addition to strengthening both benefits by four years, there is a "free" four-year spousal benefit. Full retirement age must be reached before an individual can suspend collection of his or her benefits. Again, full retirement age is age 66 for people born between 1943 and 1954. I have no idea why the government decided to allow married Social Security recipients to be treated so generously. Maybe someday they will change it, but right now, this is a grand strategy for many married couples.

This can be an enormously beneficial strategy, but it won't work for everyone. The spouses' ages and circumstances must be "right" in several ways. There are other strategies that could be more advantageous than this one, for your particular circumstances. The point of this chapter is not to give an exhaustive analysis of every Social Security strategy. Instead, the point is to show there are extremely advantageous strategies that you should know about and consider when planning your finances and even the decision to get married. As I said earlier, much will depend upon your personal circumstances.

Should the Apply and Suspend Technique Factor into a Decision to Get Married?

Doctor Dan and Baker Bob are the same age and deciding whether it would financially beneficial to marry. Doctor Dan and Baker Bob both would like to retire at the age of 62. Together, they have combined assets worth approximately $1,000,000. The couple estimates that their current annual living expenses are around $75,000 (increased annually for cost of living). During every year of his career, Doctor Dan earned the maximum amount that "counts" for Social Security. Knowing this, we can estimate the benefit he would receive if he began collecting at age 62, age 66 and age 70. Those amounts are $23,422, $31,232, and $41,226 per year respectively. During every year of his career, Baker Bob earned a more modest amount. Assume for this example that the benefit Baker Bob would receive if he began collecting at age 62, 66 and 70 are $5,000, $6,667, and $9,070 per year respectively. Doctor Dan's goals are: 1) retire immediately, and 2) make sure that funds are available to support himself and Baker Bob until the end of both of their lives. The following scenarios paint different pictures for collecting Social Security benefits.

1. The couple remains unmarried and they each collect their Social
    Security benefits at the age of 62. Baker Bob would receive $5,000 in
    benefits and Doctor Dan would receive $23,422 in benefits. As their
    trusted advisor, I would not recommend that they retire at age 62
    given their spending, but the client wants to retire now.

2. The couple gets married. Since this couple has other money available
    for living expenses, they follow my recommendation and do not
    collect Social Security benefits upon retirement at age 62. Instead,
    Doctor Dan applies for his benefits at age 66 and suspends them until
    age 70. Baker Bob can then claim the spousal benefit of one-half of
    Doctor Dan's benefits, or $15,616, starting when Baker Bob is age
    66. This is much higher than Baker Bob's own benefit, which would
    be $6,667 at that time. Because he has waited, Doctor Dan's benefits
    will grow by the 8% delayed benefit per year from 66 to 70, plus cost
    of living increases until he turns 70, thus increasing the money
    available to care for both of them in their later years.

The following graph illustrates the difference in their assets had they
remained single and collected at 62 versus getting married and using the
Apply and Suspend strategy. If both partners are alive at age 80, the

difference in their net worth will be over $440,000. If they both live to be 90, the difference in their net worth will be over 1.5 million dollars.

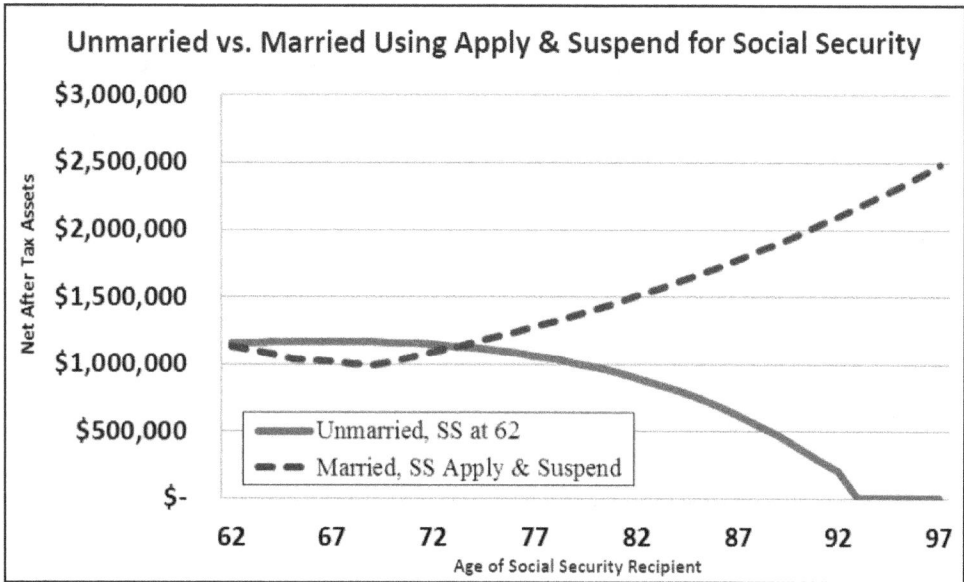

This graph reflects the following assumptions:

1. Both men were born 1/1/1952.

2. Starting date of projection is 1/1/2014, the year both partners turn 62.

3. Doctor Dan starts with $1,100,000 in after tax assets.

4. Baker Bob starts with $50,000 in after tax assets.

5. Includes a 6% Rate of Return.

6. Includes an allowance for 3% inflation of expenses, tax brackets, and Social Security.

7. Annual living expenses are $70,000 for Doctor Dan and $5,000 for Baker Bob (plus income taxes).

8. In the single scenario, Doctor Dan receives $23,422 in Social Security benefits, Baker Bob receives $5,000 plus COLAs, both at age 62.

9. In the married scenario, Doctor Dan receives maximum Social Security benefits of $41,226 at age 70 plus COLAs, Baker Bob receives 15,616 at age 66 (½ of Doctor Dan's benefits at age 66) plus COLAs.

Now, let's imagine a worst case scenario. Both Doctor Dan and Baker Bob have drafted wills, trusts, etc. saying that if something were to happen to one of them the other would inherit all the assets. Then, Doctor Dan, who used to keep his patients waiting for hours, develops cancer and dies…while waiting in the office of his oncologist. Baker Bob inherits all of Doctor Dan's assets. How long those assets will last is very different, depending on whether they married and use Apply and Suspend versus both taking their Social Security at age 62.

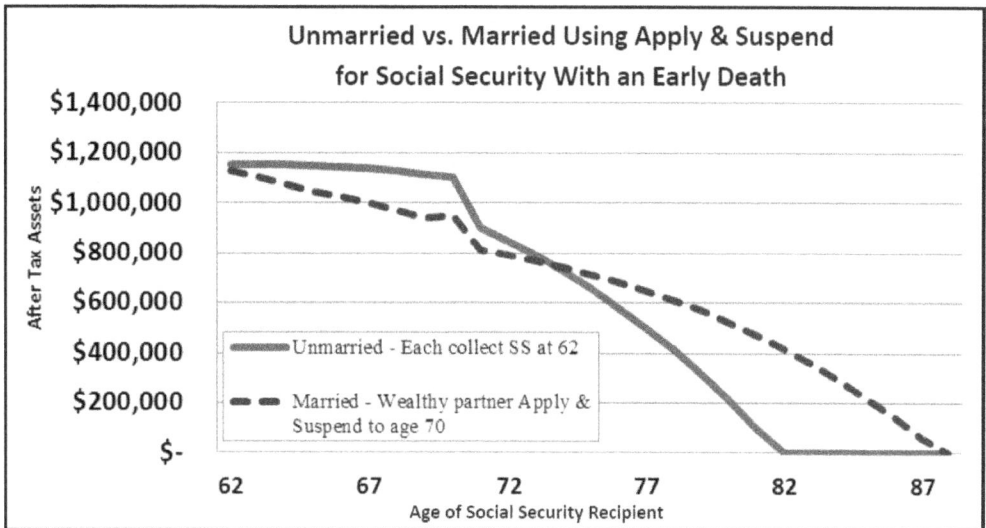

At age 82, just because the men chose to get married and use the Apply and Suspend technique, Baker Bob has a little over $400,000 in additional money to apply towards retirement.

This graph reflects the following assumptions:

1. Both men were born 1/1/1952.

2. Starting date of projection is 1/1/2014, the year both partners turn 62.

3. Includes a 6% Rate of Return.

4. Includes an allowance for 3% inflation of expenses, tax brackets, and Social Security.

5. Annual living expenses are $75,000, adjusted annually.

6. Doctor Dan dies 12/31/2022 at age 70 and leaves all his wealth to Baker Bob.

7. The current PA Inheritance Tax rate is 15%. At the date of publication, PA does not recognize same-sex marriages. When PA wakes up and joins the nationwide trend of acknowledging the rights

of same-sex couples , and we fully expect that this will occur, the following differences becomes even more significant.

8. In the single scenario, Doctor Dan receives $23,422 at age 62, Baker Bob, $5,000 at age 62.

9. In the married scenario, Doctor Dan receives maximum Social Security benefits of $41,226 at age 70 plus COLAs. Baker Bob holds off taking a spousal benefit until age 66. He then receives ½ of what Doctor Dan would have received at age 66 or $15,616 (1/2 times $31,232.) plus COLAs. After Doctor Dan dies, Baker Bob receives survivor benefits of $41,226 plus COLAs.

The blue dashed line in the chart above shows how much money will be available to care for Baker Bob if the couple remains unmarried, takes his Social Security early, and Doctor Dan dies at age 70. If he doesn't marry, and doesn't change his spending habits, Baker Bob will run out of money at the age of 82.

The red solid line represents Baker Bob's prospects if they get married and use the Apply and Suspend strategy. Baker Bob will have an additional $400,000, enough money to cover his expenses for six more years. Then, even after depleting the after-tax assets he and Doctor Dan had at retirement, he will still have a much higher Social Security benefit the rest of his life.

Notice the significant drop in after-tax assets in the year of Doctor Dan's death at age 70. This was caused by the Pennsylvania inheritance tax. Currently, this tax is assessed on same-sex partners whether they are married or not. Once Pennsylvania recognizes same-sex marriages, the inheritance tax on same-sex married couples will presumably be eliminated and the difference in this example would be even greater.

Ultimately, it would seem that the best financial strategy for Doctor Dan and Baker Bob would be to get married, delay Social Security benefits until age 66, and then use the Apply and Suspend strategy. Doctor Dan should also consider doing a series of Roth IRA conversions starting at age 62. While Roth IRA conversions are beyond the scope of this book, there are enormous benefits to doing a series of Roth IRA conversions while you are in a lower tax bracket.

Here is a summary of the basic Apply and Suspend technique:

1. At full retirement age, 66, the higher-earning spouse applies for Social Security benefits and then suspends collection.

2. The lower-earning spouse (also at full retirement age) applies for a spousal benefit.

3. At age 70, the higher-earning spouse will "unsuspend" and apply for his or her own benefit.

4. At age 70, the lower-earning spouse will either continue to collect the spousal benefit he or she has been receiving since age 66, or switch to his or her own benefit, depending on which is greater.

(As mentioned earlier, calculating the spousal benefit is more complicated if the lower earning spouse has not yet reached age 66, or if the stronger earning spouse had starting collecting before reaching 66.)

An Alternative Strategy: Claim Now, Claim More Later

There is also an alternative strategy to Apply and Suspend, in which the person with the stronger earnings record applies for a spousal benefit based on the record of the lower-earning spouse, then applies for the benefit on his/her own earnings record later (at age 70, for the maximum benefit) in order to accrue delayed retirement credits on his/her own benefit. This strategy may produce a better result than Apply and Suspend, depending on the relative ages of the spouses. That is also beyond the scope of this book, but it would be worth seeking the advice of a professional.

Summary of the Key Points and Five Strategies You Can Use To Maximize Your Social Security Benefits

The key points to remember when deciding on the timing of applying for Social Security benefits are:

1. If you apply early, your monthly benefit starts lower *and* stays lower for life.

2. Cost of living adjustments (COLA) will magnify the impact of early or delayed benefits.

3. The longer you live, the more beneficial it will have been to delay benefits.

4. Your decision to apply early or later impacts survivor benefits as well as lifetime benefits; delaying benefits may give your surviving spouse more income.

5. Spousal benefits must be taken into consideration.

There are five strategies that you can use to maximize your Social Security benefits and maximize your purchasing power. They are:

1. Improve your earnings record

2. Apply for Social Security at the optimal time

3. Coordinate spousal benefits, including the Apply and Suspend strategy

4. Minimize taxes on your benefits

5. Coordinate your Social Security benefits with other financial decisions and strategies

Let's discuss these strategies one at a time.

1) *Improve Your Earnings Record*

If you have already earned income up to, or exceeding, the Social Security wage base for 35 years, continuing to work may increase your benefit somewhat, but the increase is not likely to be substantial. If you have not been a maximum earner for 35 years, working longer will make a significant difference in your monthly benefit. The longer you work, the stronger your earnings record is going to be. I hate it when people who enjoy their work retire early so that they can get a benefit earlier. That doesn't make sense. If you like what you're doing, keep working—ultimately that's more money for you and for your spouse! I genuinely hope that all of you enjoy good health and live until a ripe old age, and it is my goal to make sure you have sufficient money to enjoy it.

2) *Apply for Social Security at the Optimal Time*

To figure out the optimal time to apply for Social Security, you must take into account your income needs, both now and in the future, your life expectancy, and your spouse's life expectancy. Suzanne, a 62 year old retiree, has a serious health problem that causes her to believe she is *not* going to make it until age 81, the theoretical "breakeven" age for Social Security using the assumptions above. She may think that she'll be lucky to make it to age 72. If she is single and not planning on getting married, Suzanne should probably apply for Social Security benefits at age 62. But, if she is married and has the stronger earnings record, she might want to wait to collect her benefits to ensure that her surviving spouse will get the higher benefit. Suzanne's health, marriage status, and estimated life expectancy are all very important parts of her analysis. What is your genetic factor? How long did your parents live? These are important questions to ask. While in general I recommend holding off, particularly for married people, sometimes it does make sense to collect early.

3) *Coordinate Your Spousal Benefits to Produce Free Money*

Consider whether you can use the Apply and Suspend strategy or the "Claim Now, Claim More Later" strategy at your full retirement age to produce "free money" over the years from age 66 to age 70.

4) *Minimize the Taxation of Your Benefits – Always a Good Idea*

There are different tax-planning techniques that will enable you to minimize income tax and also get the maximum enjoyment from your Social Security benefits. For example, even just holding off on Social Security benefits until after you're retired may keep you in a lower tax bracket. It may also produce a window of opportunity for annual Roth IRA conversions between the time you are retired and no longer receiving a paycheck, and when you turn age 70. Holding off on Social Security during those years will give you an opportunity to make larger Roth IRA conversions while you are in the lower tax brackets. Then, at age 70, when there is no advantage in holding off on Social Security, you collect the maximum benefit and you have also succeeded in making Roth IRA conversions while in the lowest tax bracket you will be in for the rest of your life. This assumes you have a substantial traditional IRA and will have to start taking minimum required distributions at age 70½. Once again, I recommend seeking the advice of a professional to coordinate Social Security and Roth IRA conversions. But it might be difficult to find a professional who really understands enough of the concepts to effectively "run the numbers." This is a niche that we have cultivated and take pride in doing well.

5) *Coordinate Your Social Security Benefits with Your Overall Retirement Income Plan*

Earlier in this chapter, I made the point that Social Security shouldn't be considered in a vacuum. There are many interrelated parts of a good financial plan. I like to integrate everything: a Social Security plan, an IRA plan, a long-term Roth IRA conversion plan, a general tax plan, an estate plan, and an investment plan. You must also take into account everything else that is going on, such as your pensions, your IRAs, your 401(k), your minimum required distributions, your working income, and your investment portfolio, and even the timing of when you should get married. What you don't want to do is to have an independent strategy for each piece of the puzzle. You want a synergistic strategy that incorporates all parts of your financial plan in concert with your life plans. And, this chapter provides compelling support for the proposition that committed same-sex couples in their sixties or older should likely get married to dramatically increase their financial security with Social Security during both of their lifetimes and after the first death.

Do you have a trusted advisor to help you with your retirement and estate planning? Do you feel confident he or she is qualified and experienced in the unique strategies that benefit same-sex couples—especially the unique strategies for couples who live in states that don't yet recognize same-sex marriage? Is your current advisor well versed in the interplay between Social Security, retirement plan distributions, and Roth conversions? If they are, great. Please, finish reading this book, list your comments and concerns, and set up an appointment as soon as possible.

If, however, you don't have a trusted advisor and can't find anyone that you feel has the appropriate expertise in integrating Social Security planning with retirement and estate planning specifically for same-sex couples, there is another option for some number of private clients who will work with me directly. I am offering a number of free consultations for qualifying residents of Western PA and taking on a very limited number of private clients who will work with me directly. I am also offering a number of paid consultations to non-Western PA residents. If you are interested in working with me and/or my firm one on one, please visit www.OutEstatePlanning.com/workwithjim or refer to the end of the book for contact information.

4

Income Tax Changes for Married
Same-Sex Couples

*Anyone may arrange his affairs so that his taxes shall be as low as
possible; he is not bound to choose that pattern which best pays the
treasury. There is not even a patriotic duty to increase one's taxes.*[14]

Judge Learned Hand

Main Topics

- Has my income tax filing status changed since the demise of DOMA?

- What are the income tax advantages and disadvantages to getting married?

Key Idea

Although it is possible to file amended returns reflecting your new legal status as

married, we strongly recommend that you "run the numbers" for married filing

jointly and compare the numbers with what you paid in taxes as two single

taxpayers—you might owe more taxes. Consult your CPA or tax advisor to determine

how changes based on your new filing status may affect you and your spouse.

How the Federal Income Tax Has Changed for Married Same-Sex
Couples

---

[14] I recently saw my college roommate, a tax attorney who fights for the other side. He
worked for the I.R.S. and now the Ohio Department of Revenue. He hates this quote.

Starting in tax year 2013, same-sex couples legally married in a state, or a foreign country, that recognizes same-sex marriage must file their federal income tax return as "married filing jointly" or "married filing separately." As of September 16, 2013, legally married same-sex couples will be considered married for federal tax purposes for the entire year. If you married on December 31, 2013, you will be considered married for the 2013 tax year. *It doesn't matter if you live in a state that does not recognize your marriage* (like Pennsylvania), for federal purposes you must file as married. The ruling *does not* apply to same-sex couples in domestic partnerships or civil unions.

The ruling applies to all federal tax provisions where marriage is a factor:

- Filing status

- Claiming personal and dependency exemptions

- Taking the standard deduction

- Claiming the Earned Income Tax credit

- Claiming the Child Care Tax credit

- Roth IRA contributions even for non-working spouses

All Legally Married Same-Sex Couples Should Review Their Federal Income Tax Returns and Make the Appropriate Changes

- Employees who must file IRS Form W-4, Employee's Withholding Allowance Certificate, should review the W-4 on file with their employer as their filing status and total number of allowances claimed has changed for federal tax purposes.

- The standard deduction will also change for legally married same-sex couples because the deduction is based on your filing status.

You must review your federal income tax return for other issues as well.

- Some income, deductions, expenses, and credits may change because of your new filing status.

- Your married filing status may change your Earned Income Tax Credit or Child Tax Care Credit as well.

- Income tax treatment of employer-provided health insurance and fringe benefits will be different now that you are considered married for federal tax purposes. Employees who purchased same-sex spouse health coverage benefits or fringe benefits that were provided by the employer and are now excludable from federal taxable income based on an individual's marital status.

That is great news. Not only that, if you paid tax on those

benefits in the past, you may file an amended return to claim a

credit or refund. Please see Chapter 6 for a review of health care

concerns.

Consult your CPA or tax advisor to determine how these and any other

changes based on your new filing status may affect you and your spouse. If

you are a do-it-yourselfer, I find the easiest ways to test different scenarios is

with tax software like Turbo Tax or Tax Cut.

Legally married same-sex couples may choose to file amended federal tax

returns for one or more prior tax years depending upon the statute of

limitations. Generally, the statute of limitations for filing a refund claim is

three years from the date the return was filed, or two years from the date the

tax was paid, whichever is later. So, refund claims can still be filed for tax

years 2010, (if you are reading this before April 15, 2014), 2011, and 2012.

- If you are a legally married same-sex couple reading this book

    between April 15, 2014 and April 15, 2015, you will have to file

    your 2013 and 2014 as either married filing jointly or married filing separately, not single. You could file amended returns for 2011 and 2012.

- If you are legally married and are reading this before April 15, 2014, you could also file an amended return for 2010.

Understand that filing an amended return is optional. Some couples might actually owe additional taxes to the IRS for previous years if they file amended returns reflecting a married status. If you are thinking of filing amended returns, we strongly recommend that you "run the numbers" for married filing jointly versus filing as two single taxpayers, and/or have a discussion as soon as possible with your CPA or tax attorney. Then, depending upon the result, either you or your CPA could file amended returns and request a refund.

Are There Good Financial Reasons to Get Legally Married?

The Advantages and Disadvantages of Marriage on Your Federal Income Tax Return

Will there be federal income tax benefits to you if you get married? It depends on your situation. If you and your partner have highly divergent incomes, marriage may be beneficial. But, for many couples, your income taxes could actually increase if you get married because of the so called "marriage penalty" that currently hurts many straight couples.

So, when is it good to get married for federal income tax purposes, and when will there be a marriage penalty?

Examples of the Marriage Bonus from Filing Jointly

If you have significantly different incomes, it is usually going to work out better to file "married filing jointly" as opposed to two single returns—a marriage bonus. The lower earner is kind of helping to reduce the tax bracket of the higher earner and that could save you a couple thousand dollars.

1) If one partner earns $80,000 and the other earns $20,000, and they file "married filing jointly" as opposed to filing single, they will save $2,000 in income taxes.

2) If one partner earns $100,000 and the other does not work, and they are "married filing jointly" as opposed to filing single, they will save $3,000 in income taxes.

Example of the Marriage Penalty from Filing Jointly

On the other hand, let's say that you both make about the same amount of money, especially when both are high-earners. The marriage penalty usually comes into play when you have two relatively equal earners. The marriage penalty could be a difference of $1,000 or $2,000, or it could be as much as a $4,000 or $5,000. And you will pay this increased amount of income taxes every single year, which can really add up to a large sum of money.

1) If both partners earn $80,000 each, and they are "married filing jointly," they will pay $4,800 more in income taxes over each filing as "single."

Maybe Marriage is a Good Idea if You are Selling Your House

Another reason to get married and file jointly is if you are planning to sell your house for a significant gain. If you are married, you get a $500,000 exemption from your capital gain, but if you are single, the exemption is only $250,000. If you're going to sell your house, and make a lot of money on the sale of the house, which would incur a higher capital gain, you are financially better off getting married. You must meet ownership and use tests and must not have excluded gain from another home in the past two years.

Your Age Might Also Factor into Your Decision

The financial advantages and disadvantages of getting married will depend upon your particular circumstances—notice the word *financial* (that is the limit of my advice!). For example, if you are a relatively young couple, the disadvantage of the marriage penalty on your income taxes might be more important to you than the Social Security and the IRA beneficiary and estate planning advantages. (See Chapter 2 for IRAs and Chapter 3 for Social Security.) On the other hand, if you are a couple in your sixties, when Social Security and estate planning become more important to you, then your particular circumstances may weigh more heavily toward getting married. We tend to work with older couples, where the advantages of the increased Social Security benefits and the much more advantageous rules regarding inheritance of IRAs and retirement plans are more compelling than any tax increases. That will obviously not be the case for everyone.

Further Financial Considerations to Have on Your Radar

Let's assume you decide to get married because of the financial benefits described in this book. Does that mean you should get married tomorrow? What if you are you thinking about a Roth IRA conversion? It might be better to do a Roth IRA conversion before you get married, in some circumstances. In others, it would be more advantageous to do a conversion after getting married. In many if not most cases, it will pay to start Roth IRA conversions for the stronger spouse after marriage, and start the financially weaker spouse's Roth IRA conversion before getting married. [(For more on Roth IRA conversions see my book, *The Roth Revolution: Pay Taxes Once and Never Again. (Morgan James, 2010)]*

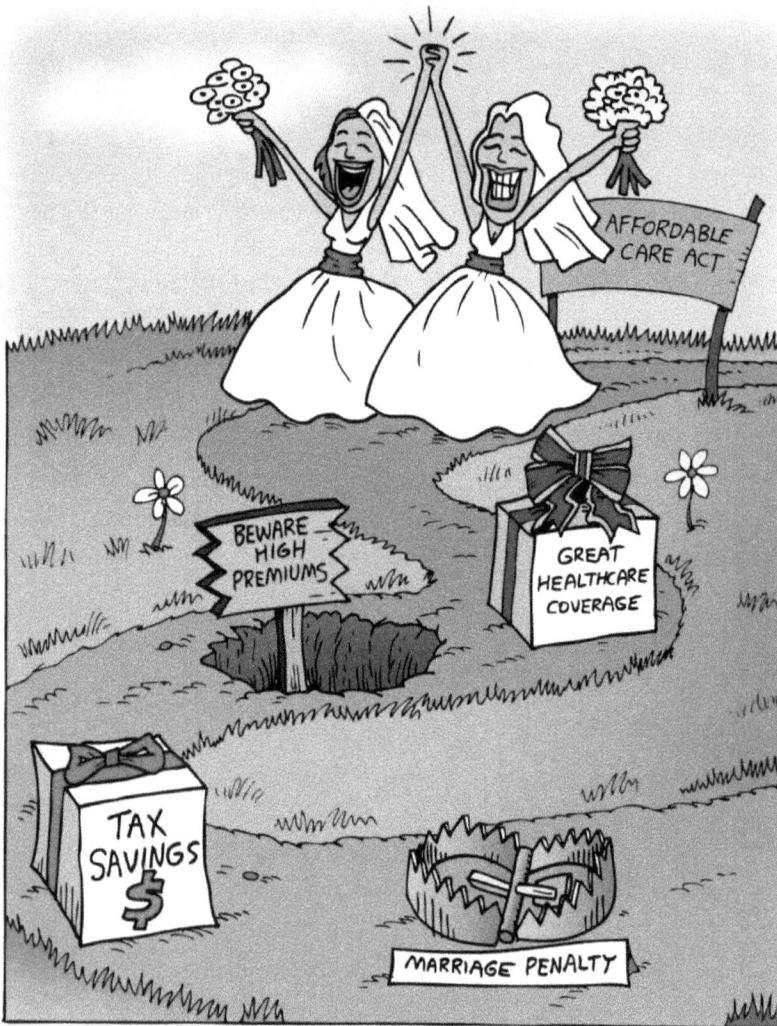

What Is Your Filing Status for State Income Tax Purposes?

Federal income tax returns calculate federal adjusted gross income (AGI) and federal taxable income, and these calculations take your filing status into account to determine your income. However, many states incorporate the federal amounts for adjusted gross income or taxable income into their state income tax returns. The situation can become complicated when the state in which you live does not recognize your marriage, but the federal government does.

- For the most part, same-sex married couples will now file their state income tax returns as married, if they live in a state that recognizes same-sex marriage. There are some exceptions. For example, some states do not have state income taxes, and some states tax only interest and dividends, not individuals.

- Most legally married same-sex couples who currently live in states that do not recognize their marriage, cannot file their state income tax returns as married. Please see http://benefitsattorney.com/charts/state-taxes-and-married-same-sex-couples/ for the rule in your state.

  - In Pennsylvania, a legally married same-sex couple will file their federal income tax return as married, but their state income tax returns as single.

  - In Oregon, a legally married same-sex couple will file their federal and state income tax returns as married.

- In Missouri, a legally married same-sex couple may file a joint state income tax return and a federal return as married.

- In Colorado, a legally married same-sex couple will file their federal and state income tax returns as married.

- In Utah, a legally married same-sex couple may file a joint state income tax return and a federal return as married.

You will likely hear a lot about the income tax changes for same-sex couples in the coming months and even years. We have tried to cover some of the critical income tax issues in this chapter. Please remember, however, for most couples, income tax avoidance or reduction (unless you count income taxes on IRA distributions after death) is not the main financial motivation to get married. The main financial motivation for most same-sex couples to get married will be the treatment of IRAs and retirement plans at death and optimizing your benefits from Social Security.

5

Trusts for Same-Sex Couples

Love all, trust a few, do wrong to none.

William Shakespeare

Main Topics

- How can I use a trust to protect my loved ones?
- Should my trust define income as a percentage of principal?

Key Idea

Attorneys love to set up trusts and they are not always appropriate. We present some controversial alternatives to trusts. If trusts are appropriate, many same-sex couples should consider some variation of the total return trust as part of their estate plan.

There is no simple answer to the question of whether using a trust in an estate plan makes sense. Their appropriateness will depend upon your situation and the nature of your relationship. But, there are some cutting-edge techniques that can be used to address some of these perplexing questions.

Providing For Your Partner or Spouse after You Die While Still

Protecting Your Own Beneficiaries (Who Are Not the Same People as Your Partner's Beneficiaries)

A number of my clients do not share the same beneficiaries. One partner[15] might have a child from a prior marriage or a prior relationship. Maybe neither partner has a child, and each partner would like their own families— brothers and sisters, nieces and nephews etc.—to be their eventual beneficiaries. And yet, the first level of concern is providing for the surviving partner or spouse. What do you do in that situation?

Well, you could provide for your partner in your will, and you could name your partner as the primary beneficiary of your IRA[16] or life insurance, and name members of your biological family as secondary beneficiaries. However, if you die with this simple designation, your partner will inherit everything if he or she is still alive when you die. This is because the secondary beneficiary designation is a Plan B – it says that your partner would be your first choice to receive the money, but if he or she isn't alive

---

[15] Rather than complicate the explanations by saying "partner or spouse" throughout, I will simply say "partner." But be assured that these strategies work whether or not you are married to your life partner.

[16] It is the beneficiary designation of your retirement accounts and of your life insurance policy (and not your will) that establishes who will inherit these assets.

when you die, then your second choice would be your family. In this scenario, your partner was alive when you died, so there was no need to look any further. Your partner inherited all of your money, and your biological family would not have received a dime. Now it will be your partner's will and beneficiary designations that control all of your money, after he or she dies. That creates the potential for all of the assets that you left your partner to go to your partner's beneficiaries—not your biological family or the particular charities that you wanted to provide for. Let's say that the money you have now was inherited from your parents when they died, and their expressed intent was for that money to be passed down to members of your biological family (their beloved grandchildren). Maybe you agree that the money should remain in the hands of members of your biological family. With the simple designation mentioned above, with your partner as number one and your biological family as number two, your partner controls your family's money upon your death—which was never your intention. That is disastrous. The standard solution is to create a trust.

How a Standard Trust Works

What are the terms of a standard trust? Usually it will be set up to say, "income to spouse, or income to partner, and at partner's death, the principal (whatever is left) returns to the biological family." Let's assume Margie has a million dollars and she tells the attorney that she wants to make sure that her partner is provided for, but after her partner dies, she wants the million dollars, or whatever is left of it, to go back to her biological family. The attorney prepares a legal document called a testamentary trust for her, which means the trust is a part of Margie's will and takes effect and remains unfunded until the time of Margie's death. The terms of the trust say that her partner will get the income from the million dollars for as long as she lives. At Margie's death, her partner does not receive the million dollars outright. The money goes to a trustee that Margie had chosen previously, and it is invested for the benefit of her partner and, ultimately, her biological beneficiaries. While Margie's partner is alive, she receives income from the trust, and then when she dies the corpus (or whatever is left) returns to Margie's biological family. It is also important to note that neither Margie's partner nor her biological family can receive money at a faster rate than what Margie had specified in her trust. So if Margie's partner had received her income as defined by the trust, but wanted an additional $40,000 to buy a new car, unless there was a provision in the will that would say otherwise, she would be out of luck.

How a Traditional Trust Defines Income

There is a problem with the average trust that revolves around the trust's definition of *income*, and in the current economic climate, the problem is even worse. Traditionally, when trusts are drafted by attorneys, the word *income* is defined as "the interest and dividends on stocks and bonds or cash investment accounts". Currently, the interest rate on many bank accounts is maybe 1% to 2%, and dividends on many investments are not much higher. So, if Margie's million dollar trust uses the standard definition of income, her partner might only receive $10,000 or $20,000 a year. That amount of money is not really going to do a great job of providing for Margie's partner, if she has no other sources of income.

Moreover, the traditional definition of "income" does not usually include *appreciation*. We've had some good years in the market recently—the index funds that we recommend to our clients are up 9.41% over ten years, after fees, and are up 27.12% in 2013. But, Margie's traditional trust makes no income accommodation for the 27.12% appreciation, or gain. The income paid to her partner is still limited to the roughly 2% garnered from interest and dividends. So, what can you do?

Use a Different Definition to Define Income

If you like the idea of a trust, but $10,000 or $20,000 will not meet your

partner's income needs, one solution is to redefine *income*. When drafting

the trust, we can drop the traditional accounting definition of income

(interest and dividends) and use a definition that makes more sense for this

individual. So, we specify that our definition of *income* means *a percentage*

of principal. And that can be 4% of principal, 5% of principal, or whatever

seems appropriate.

For this example, we will use a *4% of principal* scenario. We draft a trust for

Margie that says, "At my death, my million dollars goes into a trust. My trust

will pay 4% of the principal every year, to my partner. When my partner

dies, the corpus, or the principal of the trust, is returned to my biological

family or to my beneficiaries." It is important to understand that, because of

the trust, Margie's partner does not have access to the million dollars when

Margie dies. If the principal in the trust the first year is $1,000,000, Margie's

partner will only receive $40,000 from the trust (4% x $1,000,000). And,

because we're defining income as a percentage of principal in Margie's trust,

her surviving partner's income will likely fluctuate from year to year. Now,

hopefully the trustee that Margie has chosen invests the million dollars

wisely, for growth and appreciation. If the trust grows to $2 million, her partner's annual income from the trust would be $80,000 (4% x $2,000,000).

If things turn sour and the trust assets decline to $800,000, then her surviving

partner's income would drop to $32,000 (4% * $800,000). Either way, the

outcome is more favorable for her partner than if she had used the standard

definition of "income" for her trust. There are also formulas that could be

used to "smooth" the annual distribution of income.

A Concept Called the Total Return Trust

As much as I might like to take credit for it, redefining income from "interest

and dividends" to "a percentage of the principal" (or some variation thereof)

was not my idea. Actually, one of the pioneers of this type of trust is an

attorney in Pittsburgh, named Robert Wolf. Either he or somebody else

dubbed it a "total return trust". Bob Wolf devised this concept roughly

eighteen years ago, when income from interest was much higher. The

challenge facing the trustees at the time was how to invest the money in the

trust. If the trustee invested for income, the income beneficiaries of the trust

were happy, but the end beneficiaries weren't happy because the assets in the

trust were not growing—meaning that they'd ultimately inherit less money.

If the trustee invested for growth, the end beneficiaries were very happy

because the trust assets they stood to inherit were increasing, but the income

beneficiaries were furious because they didn't get very much money at all (remember, appreciation is not included in the standard definition of "income"). Wolf's solution, which I think was brilliant, was to define income as a percentage of principal.

Total return trusts have enjoyed tremendous growth with more enlightened law firms and banks and trust companies, though perhaps not as much as Bob Wolf would like. I borrowed Wolf's concept and applied it to my clients who were in same-sex relationships. In 2002, I put up a website called www.outestateplanning.com and wrote an article explaining why this concept was a good idea for same-sex couples. Back then, there were different reasons to use the total return trust concept. Interest rates were much higher at the time, and the trustee was being helped with a total return trust because he could satisfy both the income beneficiaries and the end beneficiaries at the same time. Now, the total return trust concept is especially important to the income beneficiary because income, in the traditional definition, is just so bad in today's low interest rate environment.

Avoiding Conflict among Beneficiaries and Other Issues

A total return trust avoids conflict between the trustee, the ultimate beneficiary, and the life-income beneficiary. With a traditional trust, there are often arguments, even lawsuits, among the various beneficiaries and the trustee over how the trust assets should be invested. Even if interest rates do increase dramatically in the next few years, you still might have some of those same conflicts between the parties of a traditional trust. The income beneficiary might want the trustee to invest for income, and the end beneficiary might want the trustee to invest for growth—and the trustee is stuck in the middle because he or she can never make everybody happy. However, if everybody has the same goal, i.e. growing the principal of the trust, *everyone* benefits. The income beneficiary will get more money, the end beneficiary will get more money, and the trustee, if his or her fee is based on how much money they are managing, will also get more money. It seems to be a win-win-win situation.

There are certainly many same-sex couples who should consider some variation of the total return trust as part of their estate plan, but trusts are not always appropriate or needed.

A Simple Solution When You Want to Provide for Your Partner and Others Heirs

A different solution, though not necessarily the best solution, is to give either specific assets, or a percentage of your assets to your partner/spouse. The remainder goes to your other heirs. For example, you could leave your Roth

IRA to your younger heirs,[17] and your after-tax investment accounts to your partner/spouse. The problem with doing this might be that, if, after time passes, you spend all of your after tax dollars, saving your Roth IRA dollars to spend last, your children will still inherit your Roth IRA but your partner will inherit nothing. The solution to that problem is to leave certain percentages of all your assets to your partner, and the remaining percent to your family or other heirs.

Life Insurance

Even if you or your attorney has the wisdom of King Solomon, sometimes there is no great answer to how you should divide up your estate between your partner and other heirs. This is particularly true when your partner is currently relying on your income, but your estate isn't big enough to provide for your partner and your other heirs no matter how you slice up the pie.

Rather than sweating over the details of dividing up the pie, another simple solution is to just make a bigger pie—with life insurance! Life insurance is uncomplicated – there are no names to change on accounts, there are no

---

[17] The idea of leaving your Roth IRA to your young heirs is to extend tax free growth for as long as possible. However, if the government changes the laws for Inherited Roth IRAs and if you are married, then leaving your Roth IRA to your spouse would allow for a longer stretch of tax free growth.

assets to sell—it can make your partner and your other heirs happy. The only unhappy one is you, since you have to pay the premium.

And, while we are on the subject of life insurance, even if you are not trying to figure out how to divide the pie, sometimes life insurance is just appropriate to provide for your partner. Even if you are leaving your entire estate to your partner, if your partner doesn't have sufficient assets to live comfortably even after inheriting your estate, you should consider making a bigger pie with life insurance.

Providing for Your Partner without Extended Family Constraints

What if providing for your partner is your primary concern?

The total return trust that I wrote about in 2002 on www.outestateplanning.com was not as popular with same-sex couples as I expected. Why? It turns out that most of my clients in same-sex relationships were primarily interested in providing for their partner, and what happened after the death of the second partner was not of great concern to them. There are a lot of problems with the total return trust. For example, what if your entire estate is $300,000 instead of a million dollars? In that case, the income, no matter how you define it, is not going to be sufficient. Also, what if you want to plan for the unexpected after the first death? What if your

partner needs more money because of health issues or other unanticipated

expenses arise?

One solution, but perhaps not the best solution, would be to change the terms

of the trust. You could include language in your trust that says, "The trustee

is authorized to invade the corpus of the trust for medical emergencies." Or,

you could say, "The trustee is authorized to invade the corpus of the trust for

health, maintenance, and support." This solution, although viable, is still not

perfect, particularly for a smaller estate that will incur the costs and

aggravation of trust administration. When you create a trust, there must be a

trustee, perhaps a bank, perhaps a person, but in either case there will be

additional tax returns, not to mention the cost of drafting the trust. Do you

really want more bankers, lawyers, and accountants to get their greedy paws

on your hard earned money instead of your partner? So, is there an

alternative to a trust?

An Alternative Solution is an Agreement with Your Partner

In this next section, I present the minority viewpoint and concede the

majority may very well be right in many if not most cases. I present my view

anyway, because for the right couple, maybe you and your partner, it can make an enormous difference and be the best estate plan there is for you.

Let's assume your *primary* concern is to provide for your partner—and if there is something left, you would like it to return to your biological family. But you don't want to do a total return trust because you don't think the income provisions, however they are defined, will provide enough income for your partner. Plus, you don't like the idea of having to choose a trustee, and the taxes and the expenses of the trust are just added complications that you'd prefer to not deal with. And you also learned in Chapter 2 that, when the underlying asset of the trust is an IRA, it can be an unmitigated income tax disaster especially if you are married, and the asset that you wanted to put in your trust, is your IRA. Let's assume you also don't like the idea of splitting it in terms of percentages because you fear if it is less than 100%, you won't sufficiently be providing for your partner.

What about a different idea? Let's assume, for the sake of discussion, that you trust your partner unconditionally. (Not everybody does by the way—so if you don't, you are not alone and this solution will not work for you.) But if you do trust your partner, how about saying this to them?

> "Here's the deal: I'm going to leave you all of my money (or at least a big chunk of it), but I want you to keep it in a separate account after

I die. You're allowed to go into that account when you need it for your own purposes or for your own support, but you keep your own money in a separate account. Legally, all of the money will be yours. But our agreement* will be that you will agree to have a clause in your will and beneficiary designations, etc. that stipulates that, whatever remains of the money that I left you, which you have been keeping in a separate account, will be returned to my biological heirs or other heirs of my choosing upon your death."

* A written agreement might add a bit of comfort.

By having an oral or written agreement with your partner, you don't incur all the complications of the requirements of a formal trust. This includes the legal considerations and cost of drafting the trust, the need for a trustee after death, the extra trust income tax return, the extra complications for the beneficiaries' tax return having to deal with a K-1, and other aggravations and legal problems of a trust. You can keep things simple, but you can only do this if you *really trust* your partner. I have done this quite a bit in my practice and I will tell you, every time, with the exception of one time, it worked beautifully. To be fair, I have done this more with straight couples in a second marriage who are providing for their second spouse, but having the second spouse agree to provide for the children of the first marriage upon their death. An oral agreement could work, but a written agreement gives greater, though not even close to perfect assurance your partner will follow your wishes after you die. The written agreement is better if, for no other reason, just to make clear what the agreement is. But, whether it is written or oral, you must trust your partner to do as you ask.

There are estate attorneys, most likely the majority of estate attorneys, who would say I am crazy to even mention these types of agreements as an option—especially an oral agreement. They would say you can't trust anyone; after a death, *things* happen. I just had Paul Hood, author of *Estate Planning for Modern Families*, on my radio show. He and other attorneys (and probably even some of your own acquaintances) could come up with stories of how a second spouse cut the children from the first marriage out of their parent's estate, in spite of the promises made by that parent to the children. Honestly, they may be right. I have not had that experience. In all but one of the situations in which I have been involved, the surviving spouse has honored the wishes of their deceased spouse. I think it is up to the attorney to describe the possibilities to the client, as well as the advantages and disadvantages of different approaches and let the client decide which option makes the most sense for them. Particularly with a long relationship when the financially stronger spouse's primary goal is to leave money to their partner/spouse, I think this idea is worth considering if there is sufficient trust.

Trust Basics and Situations When a Trust May Be Appropriate

In this chapter we went straight to the fun stuff, but, before we go too much further, we had better make sure everyone understands the basics of trusts. What is a trust? A trust is basically an agreement to have a trustee administer your assets in a way that is consistent with your wishes. Trusts can be funded either during your lifetime, or at your death. The trust agreement can be revocable, meaning that you can change it, or it can be irrevocable, meaning that you cannot change it. A testamentary trust is one that takes effect after you die. A revocable trust is a trust that is usually funded while you are alive but you can change any time you like. Basically, a testamentary trust allows you to control from the grave…sometimes not a bad idea.

As I have indicated, trusts are not always appropriate or needed. If you want to benefit your partner and your biological family, you might simply say "X percent to one beneficiary, and X percent to another beneficiary." If the underlying asset is an IRA or retirement plan, this might make perfect sense.

Other times, you may have just a small amount of money that you would like to leave to a young child. In that case, you may want to put the money into a Section 529 Plan. That way you don't have to mess around with trust fees, trustee fees, and an extra tax return. In situations where there is not that much money anyway, the Section 529 Plan may have more favorable tax implications than a trust.

Naming a Trust as the Beneficiary of an IRA

You must be very careful if you are going to name a trust as the beneficiary of your IRA. Most people do not get this right. The trust must be carefully and properly drafted. The difference between doing the trust right and doing the trust wrong can mean the difference between your beneficiary having a million dollars twenty years after your death and having nothing. Don't pay taxes now, pay taxes later. If you do it wrong, you pay taxes now. If you do it right, you're paying taxes later. If the underlying asset is an IRA or other retirement plan, a poorly drafted trust can trigger an avalanche of income taxes.

Using a Trust to Provide Protection for a Minor

The most common type of trust is a trust which is established for the benefit of a minor child. Whether it is your own child, an adopted child, a niece, or a nephew, if you are leaving an appreciable amount of money to a minor, you almost always want that money to go into a trust. Without a trust, that money gets transferred under the laws of the Uniform Gift to Minors Act. Depending on what state you live in, this means that the child will have *unlimited* access to that money at age 18 or 21. I really don't think that's a very good idea, particularly if the child is very young right now and you don't know a lot about their personality. You want to know that the child is responsible and won't go out and spend all the money right away. Some children are spendthrifts who cannot hang on to money, and need the structure of a trust well into adulthood and beyond. The trust for a minor will protect the minor from self-inflicted bad judgment, it will protect them from creditors, and it could protect their assets in the event of a failed marriage later in life. It will even protect them from irresponsible actions by the other parent, if that is an issue. I find it interesting that, even though there can be enormous complications that develop when a minor child inherits money from a deceased parent, many parents with minor children do not feel the need to prepare wills or other documents that will protect those children.

Typically, a trust for a minor might read something like this: upon my death, my minor child receives income, plus the right to invade principal for health, maintenance, and support. So in this case, the minor child would receive the interest from the trust's assets, but can also ask the trustee for additional money to cover medical bills, housing expenses, etc. The trust then goes on to read that, at age 25, we give the child a third of the principal. At age 30, we give them another third, and at age 35, we give them the balance remaining in the account and terminate the trust. The terms can vary, depending on the child and your view of the world. Some of my clients set up trusts where their children do not get any principal until they are 50 years old.

Trusts for Adult Beneficiaries

Some adults never really develop money sense. You still want to provide for them, whether they are your own children, your nieces and nephews, or even children of your partner. You may disagree with what they are doing financially—they may be goodhearted people who, for whatever reason, cannot seem to hold down a job. Maybe money goes right through their pockets, or they get involved in a bad marriage. You want to protect these people, but if you leave them money outright, there is a very good chance that the money will disappear too quickly—and there goes the safety net that you had intended to provide them.

The solution is to provide them with a trust. A trust will protect them from themselves. It will protect them from their creditors, and it will protect them from their spouse. And equally significantly, it will protect them from a *future ex-spouse*. We all know someone who has been financially devastated by a divorce. You don't want the money that you left to your adult child ending up in the hands of his or her estranged former spouse.

Giving Your Beneficiaries the Right to Disclaim[18] to Other Beneficiaries

Let's assume that you have an adult child who may eventually have his or her own children. You might want to provide your child, who is your beneficiary, with the option to "disclaim" their inheritance. Or, you could name your spouse or partner as your beneficiary, and give them the right to disclaim to your child—and then also give your child the right to disclaim to a trust for his/her child or children. By disclaiming, the first beneficiary steps aside and allows the next people in line, the second or third beneficiaries, to claim the inheritance.

For discussion's sake, let's say that you have two children, Lucy and Ricky, and they each have two children. Lucy is doing really well financially, but Ricky is just getting by and will probably need to use his inheritance. You

---

[18] I only briefly cover disclaimers here because it isn't an issue unique to same-sex couples. For a much more thorough discussion of disclaimers see *Retire Secure!* (Wiley, 2006 and 2009) which is geared towards a more general audience.

can say, "I leave my estate to my children equally, but I'm going to give each child the right to disclaim to their own kids." After your death, Lucy says, "Hey, I'm making a lot of money and I don't really need more to live on. My parent left me a lot of money in an IRA and retirement plan, and the money will be worth more to my children than it is to me. Since I'd just leave this money to them in my own will anyway I'm going to disclaim it." And if she does this, Lucy's children will receive their grandparent's IRA and retirement plan. On the other hand, Ricky might say, "Hey, I'd love to disclaim, but I just need the money." If he does this, then he receives his inheritance, and his children receive nothing. There is also a third option: take some and disclaim the rest. Disclaimers offer a lot of flexibility, and that makes them a great estate planning tool.

A Trust for a Special Needs Beneficiary

You may need a trust for a beneficiary with special needs. You may have someone in your life who is receiving (or potentially expecting to receive) some kind of government benefit, like Supplemental Security Income (SSI), or maybe they require specialty medications, or government housing. If you leave money outright to someone who is receiving government support, the government is entitled to take that money back and reimburse itself for the amount that they have already paid out in benefits. Receiving money outright can also cause a special needs beneficiary to lose any government benefits they are currently receiving—so very careful planning is needed when a special needs beneficiary is involved. And, in case you were wondering, the government will know that the beneficiary has received the money, because the beneficiary's Social Security number must be listed on your estate tax return, and on life insurance claims forms. Typically, a special needs trust says that the trustee can pay out certain things to the beneficiary, but it is worded in such a way that the government cannot appropriate the money. A special needs trust is an extremely important document for a limited population. If you have a special needs child, or special needs adult, and you want to provide for that person, a special needs trust is appropriate.

Choosing a Trustee for Your Trust

Who are you going to name as the trustee? This is a big question. Let's assume that you have multiple children, or multiple nieces and nephews, around age 35, and one of your beneficiaries is a spendthrift. You are afraid that one day the spendthrift child will end up living under a bridge. So, rather than leave this child money outright, you set up a trust for their benefit. Now the question is, who are you going to name as trustee? The traditional answer to that question was usually a bank. The problems with naming a bank as a trustee is that banks charge pretty high fees, and banks have employee turnover. There are times when you cannot avoid using a bank as trustee, but a bank is rarely my first choice.

Neither do I recommend naming an attorney as trustee. Some attorneys name themselves as trustee when they draft wills and trusts for their clients, but I believe there is an inherent conflict of interest in that scenario. Furthermore, being a trustee requires a special skill set—it requires knowing the individual very well, so that informed decisions are made with respects to their trust. Banks and attorneys usually do not know their clients that well, which is another reason why I do not like to name them as trustees. Who do I prefer to name as trustee? I usually recommend naming siblings or other family members as the trustee, not because it is the best choice, but because it is the best of the bad choices. It can be a very difficult role for a family member to fulfill, but at least the family member knew your wishes and your feelings, and is more likely to act in the beneficiaries' best interests.

Is Using a Trust a Good Idea for You?

Using a trust is a good idea when you want to provide for your partner or same-sex spouse for their life, and then ultimately return your wealth to your beneficiaries when your partner dies. This strategy assumes that you and your partner have different beneficiaries, so you should use it when you are not interested in providing for your partner's beneficiaries.

If your trust defines income as a percentage of principal, the income beneficiary (most likely your partner) will receive a fixed percentage of the balance of the trust. At his or her death, your end beneficiaries will receive the balance of the trust. The income beneficiary benefits when the corpus (principal) of the trust increases. And the ultimate beneficiaries benefit from the growing principal because, after the death of your surviving partner, they will get more money.

The other alternative, as discussed above, is having an oral or even written agreement with your partner about what will be in your partner's will regarding the money you leave your partner. This solution is the least costly and the least paper-work heavy, but it will only work if you have complete trust and faith that your partner will abide by your agreement after your death.

6

The Changing World of Health Insurance

Health is a human necessity; health is a human right.

James Lenhart, *Conversations for Paco*

Main Topics

• If I get married, will my marriage affect my eligibility for a health care tax credit?

• Can I exclude the cost of my spouse's health coverage from my gross income?

• Should I amend my prior federal income tax returns to claim a credit or refund?

• What are some of the best strategies to maximize Social Security benefits?

Key Idea

Under the Affordable Care Act, there are significant new opportunities in health care coverage and potential tax savings. You should know your new rights, but also be leery of some traps that could make getting married more expensive.

Introduction: The Affordable Care Act

The Affordable Care Act (ACA), unofficially known as "Obamacare," offers new health care insurance options for same-sex couples, as well as single gay, lesbian, bisexual and transgender individuals. Under the ACA, the health insurance marketplaces (organizations set up in each state to create markets for buying health insurance coverage through private insurance companies) are prohibited from discriminating on the basis of sexual orientation and gender identity. The ACA also prohibits discrimination in all health plans that receive federal funding.

These are most welcome developments that will have enormous implications for those most in need. Of course this health care insurance still must be purchased.

Filing Requirements for Tax Credits

Same-sex couples must remember that if they were legally married in a state that recognizes same-sex marriage, then the Affordable Care Act (Obamacare) requires them to file a joint federal income tax return to be eligible to receive tax credits to lower their health care premiums. These joint tax credits are available to all legally married same-sex couples, including legally married same-sex couples who live in a state that does not recognize same-sex marriage. These tax credits are based on your jointly filed federal income tax return. If you are not legally married, you must apply for the tax credits as an individual.

The Affordable Care Act offers a new tax credit to eligible individuals to help with health care purchases that are made through the government's Health Insurance Marketplace. Advance payments of this tax credit can be sent directly to the insurer; the tax credit is then applied towards the monthly insurance payments, resulting in lower monthly premiums. Individuals whose incomes are less than $45,960 and married couples whose joint incomes are less than $62,040 will be eligible for these tax credits to lower their health care premiums (for a complete definition of "income" see www.irs.gov/uac/Newsroom/Questions-and-Answers-on-the-Premium-Tax-Credit question number seven). This means that some same-sex partners having comparable incomes will each be eligible for federal tax credits if they are unmarried, but will not be eligible for tax credits if they are legally married. For example, let's say each partner has an individual income of $35,000, or $40,000, or even $45,000. If those partners remain unmarried, at each of those income-levels, they will be eligible for health care tax credits. However, if they legally marry, their joint income of $70,000, or $80,000, or $90,000, will make them ineligible for these tax credits because they are over the threshold allowance of $62,040 for joint taxpayers. In situations where unmarried partners have disparate incomes, let's say one partner has an income of $90,000 and the other has an income of $20,000, the lower-earning partner will be eligible for health care tax credits. But, if the couple gets married their joint (combined) income will make them ineligible for these tax credits. However, if they marry and file a joint federal income tax return, the couple may benefit from falling into a lower tax bracket and this would offset the fact that they are not eligible for health care tax credits. As we frequently recommend, it is critical to run the numbers when multiple variables come into play.

New Tax Regulations for Employer Provided Health Care Plans for Same-Sex Couples

Let's assume you work for a company that is progressive enough to offer same-sex spousal benefits. Before the Supreme Court ruling striking down part of the Defense of Marriage Act (DOMA), even if an employee's health care plan at work covered their same-sex spouse and that spouse was enrolled in the employer's health plan, the employer was required to calculate the fair market value of the spousal benefit and add that amount to the employee's federal taxable income—it was considered income. The employee was taxed on the value of the spousal benefit. And, in most instances, the part of the health care premium paid by the employee for his or her spouse was also taxed. The portion of the health insurance premium paid by the employer for the spousal benefit, and the portion of the health care costs that were paid by the employee for the spousal benefit were both treated as taxable income. But the new ruling has changed this calculation. The value of the spousal benefit will no longer be added to the employee's federal taxable income. In fact, in most cases, the entire premium will not be subject to federal income tax.

In addition, an employee can now make pre-tax contributions to a Section 125 Cafeteria Plan on behalf of a same-sex spouse. A cafeteria plan allows participants to receive certain benefits on a pre-tax basis. Health care costs for married same-sex couples can be paid out of pre-tax cafeteria plan dollars. The amount that the employee pays for spousal coverage is excluded from the employee's gross income and is not subject to federal income or federal employment taxes. Before the DOMA decision, same-sex spousal benefits could not be treated on a pre-tax basis. Now, a same-sex spouse is also eligible for federally tax-free reimbursements for medical expenses from an employee spouse's Health Savings Account (HSA), Flexible Spending Account (FSA), or Health Reimbursement Arrangement (HRA). The tax savings from combinations of these provisions can easily add up to thousands of dollars. Your tax savings will vary and depend upon such factors as the cost of the health care coverage for your spouse, the medical expenses incurred by your spouse, and your current tax bracket.

In the income tax chapter we mentioned that same-sex married couples have the option of filing amended tax returns for prior years if they do the calculations and find that it is to their benefit to file a joint return. You can also file an amended return to retroactively claim a credit or refund if you purchased same-sex spouse health coverage benefits or fringe benefits that were provided by your employer, as they are now excludable from federal taxable income if you are a legally married same-sex couple. The employee can also claim a refund for any relevant federal employment taxes that were paid under the old law. For example, your share of Social Security tax and Medicare tax that was assessed on a higher wage base because health care costs for your same sex spouse were included instead of being properly excluded from your wages subject to Social Security tax and Medicare tax should qualify for a tax refund. Such exclusions from gross income may put you in a lower tax bracket. Generally, the statute of limitations for filing a refund claim is three years from the date the return was filed or two years from the date the tax was paid, whichever is later. As a result, refund claims can still be filed for tax years 2010, 2011, and 2012. If you are reading this book between April 15, 2014 and April 15, 2015, presumably you will have to file your 2013 and 2014 as either married filing jointly or married filing separately, not single. You would have the option of filing amended returns for 2011 and 2012. If you are reading this before April 15, 2014, you would also have the option to file an amended return for 2010.

Filing an amended return as married might or might not be to your advantage. We recommend you "run the numbers" both ways and/or have a discussion as soon as possible with your CPA or tax attorney about taking advantage of this ruling. Understand that filing an amended return is optional. Some couples might actually owe additional taxes to the IRS for previous years if they were required to file reflecting a married status. A conversation with your tax advisor, followed by a tax assessment for "married filing jointly" versus filing as two single taxpayers would be sensible. Then, depending upon the result, either you or your CPA could file amended returns and request a refund.

A number of other protections are available to same-sex couples as well. For example, hospitals must allow visitation by a same-sex partner. Same-sex spouses must be afforded the same treatment as opposite-sex spouses for long-term care, such as nursing home care under Medicaid. Same-sex couples have the same rights as others to name a representative to make medical decisions on a patient's behalf.

The Financial Implications of Marriage on Same-Sex Health Insurance Options

Please, don't jump to the conclusion that getting married will save taxes on health care premiums in all situations—there are negative financial implications as well—it comes back to running the numbers. For instance, our firm has at least one couple who is choosing not to get married now because the financially dependent partner (the partner with a much smaller income) can get inexpensive health insurance through Obamacare. The couple would lose that inexpensive health care option if they got married because their joint income would make them ineligible. The financially independent partner has health care through her work—but the company she works for does not offer health care benefits for same-sex couples. For this couple, between the marriage income tax penalty (see Chapter 4) and the additional cost of the higher health care premium, there are substantial financial advantages to remaining unmarried—at least for the time being. Their plan is to wait until the financially dependent partner qualifies for Medicare, and then get married. That strategy might work out well. On the other hand, it could be a disastrous tax decision if the financially stronger partner dies before they get married. For instance, the surviving partner would have to pay the income taxes on her Inherited IRA and those taxes could exceed the health care premium savings. It might be a "penny wise and pound" foolish decision.

Deciding if it makes financial sense to get married is sometimes clear-cut, but sometimes not. You have to weigh the objective advantages and disadvantages; then, at least, you will know where you stand. What we are trying to do with this book is point out some of the objective criteria so that you can make informed financial decisions.

7

Federal and State Gift, Estate,
and Inheritance Taxes

To tax and to please, no more than to love and be wise, is not given to men.

Edmund Burke

Main Topics

- Defining transfer taxes

- Contrasting regulations for federal and state taxes

- Gifting as a way to avoid inheritance taxes

- Staying on top of state regulations

Key Idea

Legally married same-sex couples living in states that do not

recognize their marriage might want to consider gifting strategies

and co-ownership of assets to avoid transfer taxes.

An Overview of Transfer Taxes

Estate and inheritance taxes are imposed on the *transfer* of a taxable estate

after a person dies. Gift taxes are imposed while the owner of the property is still alive. Generally, whether an inheritance tax is imposed depends upon

the relationship of the heir or beneficiary to the deceased. The taxes can be

imposed at both the federal and the state level.

Please note that every year we routinely file a Form 1040 income tax form.

But that is based on income, not on transferring assets from one person to

another. Transfer taxes are a separate beast and should be treated and

thought of differently than income taxes. Frankly, reducing income taxes is

far more important for the vast majority of our readers, but we need to cover

transfer taxes for completeness and because there are new opportunities for

reducing transfer taxes in light of the DOMA decision and its aftermath.

Generally, an inheritance tax rate is calculated separately for each heir based

on what they receive and how the beneficiary is related to the deceased

person. On the other hand, an estate tax is imposed on the entire value of the

estate of the deceased person, but it is still necessary to consider the

relationship of the beneficiary to the deceased.

For federal tax purposes, every legally married U.S. citizen is entitled to an

unlimited marital deduction for receiving gifts or money transferred at the

death of his or her spouse. That means you could give or leave your spouse a billion dollars, and there would not be one cent of gift or estate tax. Beyond

that, there is a $5,340,000 exemption from gift and/or estate taxes for

individuals and a $10,680,000 exemption for married couples.

But, even forgetting the exemption for married couples, very few individuals

will have federal gift or estate tax worries because most people will have less

than $5.34 million. But, for those of you who might have a federal estate

and/or gift tax problem, the DOMA decision grants marital status and an

unlimited marital deduction to married same-sex couples no matter where

they live, as long as they were married in a state that recognizes same-sex

marriages. That is a new development and something enormously important

for couples who might have federal gift and/or federal estate tax problems.

At the state level, multiple states impose their own estate tax or inheritance

tax which can inflict significant financial burdens on same-sex couples living

in non-recognition states. Married same-sex couples who live in recognition

states (who leave or give their property and money to each other) don't face

similar problems because all states that assess a transfer tax also have an

unlimited marital deduction.

Married same-sex couples living in non-recognition states, however, are only exempt from *federal* gift and estate taxes, and are still subject to *state* gift, estate, and inheritance taxes. At the present time, there are four non-recognition states that impose a state inheritance tax, a state estate tax or a state gift tax on spouses of same-sex couples, but not on spouses of straight couples. Kentucky, Nebraska, and Pennsylvania have a state inheritance tax with a spousal exemption. North Carolina has an estate tax with an unlimited marital deduction. Unfortunately, married same-sex couples residing in these non-recognition states will not be able to take advantage of these spousal exemptions. However, many states have legislated changes to their inheritance and estate tax laws in the past few years, so you should consult with your tax advisor or a local attorney regarding the current laws in your state.

Gifting Between Spouses in Non-Recognition States Can Eliminate Inheritance Taxes

Most people don't like to give away their money or their property, even to their spouse, to reduce taxes at their death. But it might be advisable in some circumstances. There is no federal gift tax imposed on married couples gifting money to one another. There are only two states that impose a gift tax on gifting to someone who is not your spouse, but fortunately they both recognize same-sex marriage. So gifts can be given from one spouse to another without any federal or state transfer taxes. If you have complete faith that you and your spouse will stay together, and you think you may die within a few years, you might consider gifts to reduce inheritance taxes. For example, in Pennsylvania, transfers from one person to another that are made more than one year prior to death will escape the 15% state inheritance tax applicable on transfers to *non-relatives or by Pennsylvania standards, your same-sex spouse.* Accordingly, it is possible under specific circumstances that gifting between spouses in same-sex marriages can reduce the assessment of the Pennsylvania inheritance tax.

While gifting is a good planning option for many same-sex married couples, you must pay attention to the gift tax and death tax laws of your state. Although Pennsylvania allows transfers made more than one year prior to death to escape the inheritance tax, in other states only transfers made more than two or three years prior to death will escape taxation. As always, please see your tax advisor or a local attorney regarding the laws in your state.

Additional Gift Considerations

It is also important to consider the cost basis of assets, and the loss of step-up in basis on highly appreciated assets that are transferred by gift to the same-sex spouse rather than inherited by the same-sex spouse. Finally, it may be advisable to consider transferring assets into a jointly held account to reduce inheritance taxes by half.

I must stress that a gifting strategy is a viable option for relatively few couples. The older, richer and sicker you are, the more appropriate it is to consider gifting. Gifting can work for legally married same-sex couples who live in a state that does not have a gift tax but does have an inheritance or estate tax. However, you must trust your spouse beyond a shadow of a doubt if you are going to gift away part of your money or other property. Furthermore, you must know how many years prior to death that transfers will escape your state's inheritance or estate tax. Using careful tax planning with a knowledgeable advisor or local attorney in your state, this strategy can work for some same-sex couples. Many states that have their own inheritance or estate tax also have rules in place regarding transfers in contemplation of death, so working with a professional who knows the law in your state is imperative.

If you live in a non-recognition state, it is extremely important to keep abreast of the laws regarding same-sex marriage in your state. The same-sex marriage laws in your state may change by popular vote, by legislation, or by court decision. You should always be proactive in your tax and estate planning, whether you live in a recognition state or a non-recognition state. When the law changes in your state, you should consult your tax advisor or a local attorney to revise your tax and estate plan accordingly. However, until the law in your state changes, there are strategies available to married same-sex individuals who want to leave all of their assets to their spouse when they die without paying state inheritance and estate taxes, just like married straight couples.

8

Putting All the Pieces Together

The whole is greater than the sum of its parts.

Aristotle

Main Topics

• Steps to combine multiple strategies to reduce taxes

• Recommendation to read *The Roth Revolution* for details on Roth IRAs and Roth conversions.

• Synergy between timing Social Security benefits and Roth IRA conversions.

• Life altering variations on the life stories of Dr. Dan, Baker Bob, and Penniless Perry

---

Key Idea

No *one* key unlocks the treasure of financial security and getting

the most out of what you've got; the solution is more like a

combination lock where you have to get a lot of things right to

maximize your assets and financial security.

In Chapter 2, I demonstrated the difference between inheriting an IRA from

a non-married partner as opposed to a spouse, and showed you that the tax benefits of being married can be enormous if you inherit an IRA or

retirement plan from your spouse. In one example from Chapter 2,

PUTTING ALL THE PIECES TOGETHER

the survivor was better off by $380,000, with the only difference being that

he married his partner before his partner died. The entire difference was

attributed to the different tax treatment of the IRA at the death of the IRA

owner, who was the first to die in our example.

In Chapter 3, I demonstrated the potential increase in Social Security benefits

that a married couple can receive, especially if they use the Apply and

Suspend strategy. The difference there amounted to an additional $1,500,000

for the surviving spouse—there are no Social Security spousal benefits if you

are not married. Now we are going to present a comprehensive picture of the

benefits of combining the individual strategies; offering the combination

number to the lock, so to speak.

The basic steps:

1) Get married in a state that recognizes same-sex marriage,

   regardless of where you live (Chapter 1).

2) Name your *spouse,* not your *partner*, as the beneficiary of your

   IRAs and retirement plans (Chapter 2).

3) Take advantage of the spousal benefits for Social Security, and

   use Apply and Suspend if appropriate (Chapter 3).

4) Do a series of Roth IRA conversions over a number of years,

   preferably during low income years that are typically between the

   year you retire and the year you turn age 70 ½(when you have to

   start taking required minimum distributions (RMD) from your

   traditional IRA and/or retirement plan).

The topic of Roth IRA conversions is so important that I wrote an entire book devoted to just that subject – it is called *The Roth Revolution – Pay Taxes Once and Never Again* (Morgan James, 2011). I wrestled with the question of whether to include a Roth IRA conversion analysis in this book because I think it is such a crucial element of planning for most IRA and retirement plan owners. The reason we didn't include an in-depth analysis of the subject in this book is that Roth IRA conversions are not really an issue specific to same-sex couples. I think in order to have a complete retirement and estate plan, all IRA owners should at least consider whether a Roth IRA conversion is appropriate for their situation. If it is appropriate, then the next question is when, and how much. So, for our "putting all the pieces together" conclusion, we include the ideal timing and amount of a Roth IRA conversions analysis, without showing all the advantages in a chapter dedicated specifically to Roth IRA conversions.

The "running the numbers" process we used to arrive at our ideal timing and amount of Roth IRA conclusions is described in the appendix, but is similar to the process used when running the numbers on IRAs and Social Security in previous chapters. Unfortunately, there are more variables and complexities than with either the IRA analysis or the Social Security analysis. I fear that this book is too complex as it is. In addition to writing a book, I have made an 8 hour presentation mainly about the intricacies of Roth IRA conversions. I ask you to take that leap of faith with respect to my Roth IRA conversion numbers, because I decided not to present all the analysis. Again, our previously published Roth IRA book would be a wonderful source to get a better understanding of Roth IRAs and Roth IRA conversions.

And in case you are wondering if I am qualified to make these determinations, please know that, in 1998, I wrote and published the very first peer reviewed Roth IRA conversion article. It tied for "Best Article of the Year" in the tax journal published by the American Institute of CPAs, the *Tax Adviser*.[19] So you could say that I am the one of the pioneers of this strategy. Both my dedicated Roth IRA book and general IRA book, *Retire Secure!* received glowing testimonials from the nation's top IRA experts. In short, the same methodology and reasoning that survived that peer review process in 1998 went into the Roth IRA conversion optimization calculations that I have used here.

---

[19] "IRAs After the TRA' 97 What Hath Congress Roth?" American Institute of Certified Public Accountants' *The Tax Adviser*, May 1998.

Let's go back to our combination lock analogy. Although there is a benefit to analyzing Social Security and Roth IRA conversion strategies independently, we believe there is a synergy between Social Security and Roth IRA conversions and that they should be implemented in conjunction with one another. And what I am going to illustrate below is the synthesis of my research.

In the graph below, we compare the same two couples with identical finances, but different strategies.

The first couple

1. doesn't get married

2. both partners take Social Security at age 62

3. neither partner makes Roth IRA conversions

The second couple

1. does get married

2. uses the Apply and Suspend strategy at age 66 for Social Security

3. makes a series of Roth IRA conversions optimized per above

    discussion

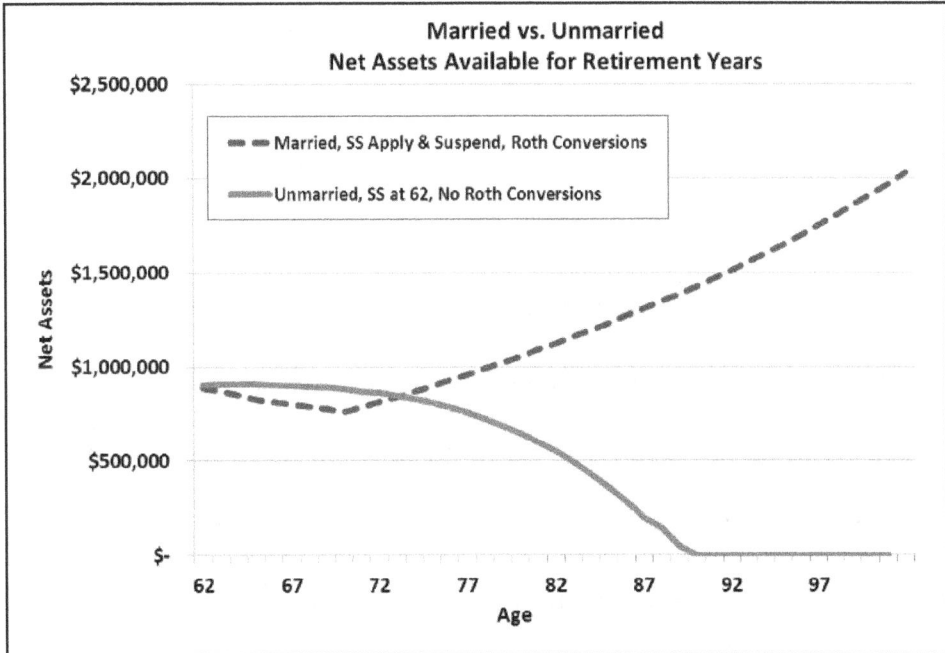

A Case Study Spanning the Later Years of Life for a Same-Sex Couple

Let's go back to the couple we've been discussing throughout these chapters,

Doctor Dan and Baker Bob. For this example, both men are age 62 when

Doctor Dan decides to retire. For income during his retirement, Doctor Dan

has his Social Security benefits, a traditional IRA with a balance of

$700,000, and after-tax savings account worth $350,000. Baker Bob has a small savings account with a balance of $50,000.[20] The men estimate that

their annual living expenses are $75,000. Doctor Dan pays a substantial

portion of those expenses, $70,000 and Baker Bob pays the balance of

$5,000.

Until retiring at the age of 62, Doctor Dan earned a reasonable living. His

earnings record is high enough that, once retired, he is able to collect the

maximum Social Security benefit possible for someone who is 62. As an

unmarried person, he could collect $23,422 per year, if he chooses to apply

for benefits at age 62. But if he waits until age 66 to apply, he could collect

$32,232 per year [plus cost-of-living adjustments (COLA) from 2014]. Now

suppose that he and Baker Bob follow my recommendation to get married,

---

[20] For our math wizards reading this, you already may be adding the numbers in your head:
$700,000 + $350,000 + $50,000 = $1,100,000 in total retirement savings. Why does our
graph start at a beginning value lower than $1,100,000 you might ask? Well, I'll tell you.
Our couple must pay income tax on any funds withdrawn from the IRA account. For the
purpose of this example, we have assumed that the income tax rate on those withdrawals to
be 28%. This reduces the available assets in the IRA from $700,000 to $504,000. It is not
that they are withdrawing the money from the IRA and paying all of the taxes. Subtracting
the taxes is just a way of showing the purchasing power of the money in the IRA. Now take
the $504,000 + $350,000 + $50,000 = $904,000. That's where our graph

begins. During the course of Doctor Dan's career he saved an additional $350,000 which is
held in a traditional brokerage account. The money invested in this account was already
after-tax money. As with most brokerage accounts, he has earned interest and dividend
income on that account, and paid any related income taxes throughout the years. Therefore,
there was no need for us to make an income tax allowance for those funds or for the cash
sitting in Baker Bob's savings account.

and they use the Apply and Suspend strategy for his Social Security. Doctor Dan would apply for benefits at age 66, and then "suspend" collecting until age 70. When he finally begins to collect, he would earn an extra 8% *each year*—or $41,226 annually (plus COLAs)—on his Social Security benefits.

Baker Bob has held down a few part-time jobs over the years, but he is primarily responsible for their home life. Assuming he does not marry, Baker Bob will be able to collect only *$5,000* each year in Social Security benefits, based on his own earnings record – and that assumes he starts to collect at age 62.   Now let's look at what happens if he and Doctor Dan marry and Doctor Dan uses the Apply and Suspend technique. If Baker Bob waits till age 66 to apply, he will be able to collect a spousal Social Security benefit of $15,616 (one half of what Doctor Dan could collect at age 66) plus COLAs. Keep in mind that Baker Bob is not eligible to receive a spousal benefit unless they are in a *legally recognized* marriage. (For the time being, they must live in a state that recognizes same-sex marriages, but we think that will soon change.)

Finances for this Couple While They are Both Living—Using All of the Advice in this Book

Now that we've gotten all of the details out of the way, let's review the results of the graph above. You can see that, from ages 62 to 70, if the men are married and they take our other advice, their assets decrease more rapidly than if they had remained unmarried and begun taking Social Security. There are two reasons for this, and the first should be obvious. Doctor Dan retired at age 62 and his income plummeted to zero. The second reason is that they have deliberately chosen to not collect Social Security benefits for the years they are ages 62 to 66 –instead, they're going to withdraw some money from Doctor Dan's after-tax brokerage account to live on. Doctor Dan takes my advice, and applies for and suspends his Social Security benefits at age 66, while still allowing Baker Bob to collect his spousal benefits from the ages of 66 to 70. Doctor Dan waits until age 70, and then takes his full increased amount of Social Security. By delaying until age 70, he reaps the additional benefit of the 8% interest per year (plus COLAs) that has been accruing since he was age 66. As demonstrated in Chapter 3, there would have been significant benefits even if he had only held off collecting his Social Security until age 66, but holding off until age 70 is the optimal choice for him. Baker Bob's ability to collect a spousal benefit at age 66 that is based on Doctor Dan's higher earnings record, and Doctor Dan's ability to collect full Social

Security benefits at age 70 rapidly makes up for the decrease in assets experienced in the early years. After only 10 years, the benefits of this approach far exceed the other alternative.

In order to strengthen their overall financial position, Dan made a series of Roth IRA conversions between age 62 and age 70. With our guidance, Dan converted the maximum amount he was able to receive as "income", without pushing the couple into a higher income tax bracket.

This brings us to one of the reasons that you have to look at these issues synergistically. A side benefit to Doctor Dan's Roth IRA conversions is that they lower Doctor Dan's RMD (required minimum distribution) from his traditional IRA, because the amount of money in the traditional IRA is reduced. A further benefit of the Roth conversion strategy is that the lower RMD at age 70 and beyond cut Doctor Dan's income taxes when he is in his highest income tax bracket. If Doctor Dan needs to withdraw money from the Roth IRA, he can do so without worrying about income tax implications. If he doesn't withdraw anything from the Roth IRA, Doctor Dan, Baker Bob, and Penniless Perry will all benefit from the income-tax free growth on the account (assuming he predeceases them).

We can now understand that the decrease in assets for the married couple in our graph is caused by them living on nothing but after tax assets from the age of 62 to 70.

The chart takes a significant bend upwards when both men reach the age of 70. Baker Bob continues to collect Social Security benefits based on a spousal benefit on Doctor Dan's earnings, but now Doctor Dan also begins collecting benefits at the increased rate we discussed previously. At age 70½, Doctor Dan must begin taking RMDs from what remains of his traditional IRA. Since the balance of his traditional IRA account has been decreased by the Roth conversions done prior to his age 70, the amount of his required RMD is reduced.   This in turn reduces the amount of income tax payments due. Doctor Dan's initial RMD starts around $35,000. Add to that both men's Social Security benefits of $41,226 and $15,616. These three items alone total $91,842, which is more than enough income to cover their annual living expense of $75,000. (Keep in mind that all of these numbers are based on today's dollars, and would be increased for COLAs. The graph takes those adjustments into account.) Since 100% of their living expenses are met, the balance of savings in both IRA accounts continues to grow throughout their lives.

Now let's take a look at the other scenario on the graph, where the men remain unmarried. Doctor Dan retires at 62, both men begin to collect Social Security benefits immediately based on their individual earnings record, and they make no Roth IRA conversions. At first, their combined Social Security benefits of $28,422 ($23,422 plus $5,000) help to cover a portion of the cost of their annual living expenses of $75,000, but they must still withdraw funds from their after-tax savings account to meet their budget requirements. (Once again, keep in mind that all of these numbers are based on today's dollars and would be increased for COLAs. The graph takes those adjustments into account.) Neither "single" man has to make any income tax payments from the ages of 62 to 69, which also helps to minimize declining assets. However, at age 70, we can see the "unmarried" line on the graph begin dropping at a more rapid pace. This is created by the income tax payments due on the higher RMDs that Doctor Dan must take starting at age 70½.

Had he transferred funds from his traditional IRA into a Roth IRA in those early years of retirement, his RMDs would have been reduced which, in turn, would have reduced his income tax payments. In addition, the only increase in Social Security benefits either of these men will see results from the annual cost of living adjustments. From the very beginning of their retirement, the unmarried couple must use a portion of their after-tax savings in order to cover their annual living expenses. By the age of 90, the men will have completely wiped out their after-tax savings and their IRA, and will have nothing but their reduced Social Security benefits as a means for financial support. If Doctor Dan dies first, his Social Security benefits will cease, and Baker Bob will spend the rest of his life living well below the federal poverty level.

On the other hand, if they take my advice to 1) get legally married, 2) Apply and Suspend Social Security at age 66 and take spousal benefits for Baker Bob, and 3) do Roth IRA conversions from age 62 to age 67, their spendable assets will continue to increase. At age 70, the men would have an additional $125,000 in spendable assets. At age 80, their assets grow to $406,000 and, at age 90, they'll have $1,427,000. If one of them lives beyond age 90, there would be an even greater difference. And it doesn't matter at which age they die—they would still be able to leave a healthy nest egg for Baker Bob's son, Penniless Perry.

Which of these scenarios would you rather see happen for you and your own partner?

Let's Take Our Case Study to the Next Phase in Life—the Death of One Spouse/Partner

We know that Doctor Dan is self-sufficient. If he takes my advice and invests responsibly, presumably using a well-diversified set of low cost index funds, he will be able to support himself and Baker Bob for as long as he lives. Unfortunately, we also know that Baker Bob has limited funds, and his own earnings record entitles him to a meager Social Security benefit. Baker Bob will not be able to support himself if something happens to Doctor Dan and he has to rely on his own resources. Even though Doctor Dan plans to leave all his assets to Baker Bob, he is still worried about his partner and wants to take all the appropriate steps to maximize Baker Bob's financial security if he predeceases him. Although this should not come as a shock, the advice we gave Doctor Dan to benefit both he and Baker Bob while they are both alive will make an even bigger difference to Baker Bob if Doctor Dan predeceases him. Refer to "A Case Study Spanning the Later Years of Life for a Same-Sex Couple" (above) to see the specifics of our partners prior to Doctor Dan's death.

The chart below displays the three possible scenarios: (1) married with the couple having followed all my strategic advice; (2) remaining unmarried and not following any of my advice (under existing laws related to *Inherited*

IRAs); and (3) the unmarried scenario using the likely future laws governing

Inherited IRAs (a total of five years to distribute the *Inherited IRA*).

Finances for the Surviving Partner/Spouse—Using All of the Advice in this Book

Let's run the numbers again comparing "taking my advice" and "not taking

my advice." This time we are assuming that one partner dies. We will

compare the same benefits that we discussed in the previous scenarios:

getting married versus remaining unmarried and the effects on the IRA;

Applying and Suspending at age 66 versus taking Social Security at age 62;

and rolling a traditional IRA into a Roth IRA during the transitional years

between age 62 and 70 versus keeping all money in the traditional IRA.

Keep in mind that all of our current scenarios are a direct continuation of our

previous scenarios. Previously we tracked the growth or loss of the couple's

assets assuming the men lived beyond 100 years. For this scenario we are

simply taking the previous accounts to the end of their 78th year, when

Doctor Dan dies. All balances at that point are going to be inherited by Baker

Bob.

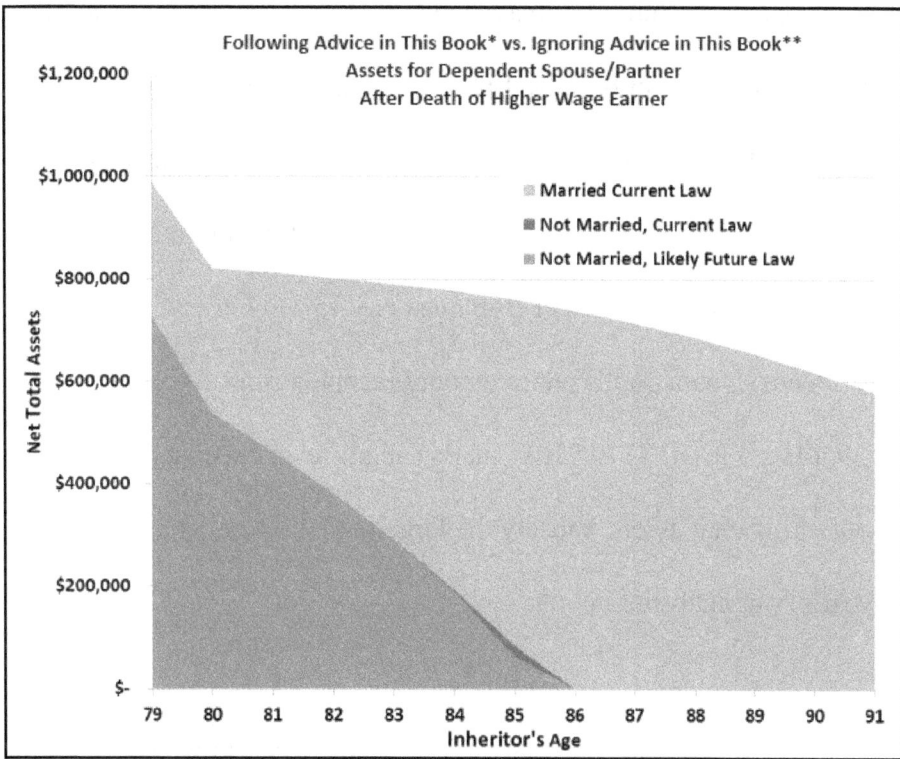

Following Advice in This Book* vs. Ignoring Advice in This Book**
Assets for Dependent Spouse/Partner
After Death of Higher Wage Earner

The top line on our graph represents the married and widowed Baker Bob. At the age of 79 he receives an inheritance from his husband, Doctor Dan of $1,139,402 (unadjusted for income tax). The inheritance consists of a Roth IRA totaling $603,405 and a traditional IRA of $535,997.[21]

---

[21] Again for our math wizards: yes, Baker Bob inherited $1,139,402. So why does our graph start below $1,000.000? Let me explain. We start our calculation with Baker Bob's inheritance excluding any income tax implications. We must do this because we have to calculate the Inheritance Tax on the entire balance of the inheritance. But for the balances carried forward on our graph, we want to reduce the traditional IRA by the 28% income tax assumption to calculate its actual purchasing power. So our beginning balance is calculated as follows: Roth $603,405 + (Traditional IRA $535,997 – $150,079 [28% tax]) = $989,323. This is the starting point of our graph.

The graph shows a rapid drop in assets in the *very first year* after Doctor Dan's death, and it's not because Baker Bob has gone on a wild spending spree. Even though he was legally married to Doctor Dan, the state of Pennsylvania (where our couple resides) does not currently recognize same-sex marriages. Therefore, Baker Bob must pay 15% inheritance tax to the state of Pennsylvania on the entire amount received from Doctor Dan ($1,139,402 x 15% or $170,910). That's a significant expense that must be paid out of his total assets, causing the large reduction of net assets in the first year of our analysis.

After the first year in the "Married Current Law" scenario we can see the relatively slow reduction in assets. This is a result of the married couple taking advantage of all the advice I suggested for the years between age 62 and the year Doctor Dan passed away. This provided Baker Bob with over $300,000 more in spendable assets *from the very first day of his inheritance,* as compared to the unmarried scenario. And that is only the first of several advantages from which Baker Bob will benefit, simply because the couple married. Baker Bob will also receive:

1. higher Social Security benefits based on his spouse's benefits after Doctor Dan

Applied & Suspended his benefits at 66, or $41,226 (plus

COLAs)

2. the advantage of the tax free Roth IRA distributions

3. the advantage of the RMD rules for rolling over a spousal IRA.
    (As we saw in Chapter 2 this benefit alone, in contrast to the
    draconian rules for a non-spouse beneficiary might be enough to
    justify marriage.)

Between the ages of 62 to 67, Doctor Dan rolled a significant amount of
money from his traditional IRA into a Roth IRA. This means that Doctor
Dan paid the income tax up front on those rollovers, which in turn reduced
the balance of the traditional IRA and the amount of inheritance tax Baker
Bob had to pay on it when he died. It also allows the $603,405 balance in the
Inherited Roth IRA to grow tax free, and to be withdrawn tax free. And
because the couple married, Baker Bob is able to roll Dr. Dan's IRA into his
own IRA, which will allow for lower RMDs and lower income tax
payments.[22] Ultimately, if the couple marries, Baker Bob will have more
than enough assets to support himself to the end of his life. If he dies at age
90, Baker Bob will still have spendable assets of $618,697.

I think most readers find this confusing, and have difficulty understanding

---

[22] Based on the Uniform Life Table IRS Publication 590.

why the assets vary so greatly between the Married and Lives graph (left

with $1,427,000 at age 90) compared to the Married and Dies graph (left

with $618,697 at age 90), so I want to explain why that happens. After

Doctor Dan dies, Baker Bob must pay state inheritance tax the very next

year. He has no other money, so he must take money from his rolled over

IRA to pay that tax. The second year after Doctor Dan passes, Bob must now

pay federal income taxes on the large distribution he took from his IRA the

previous year, to pay the state inheritance taxes. Those two tax payments

drop the balance in his IRA quite significantly, by $218,910 ($170,910

Pennsylvania Inheritance Tax + $48,000 Federal Income Tax). Baker Bob

also loses the annual investment income of $13,135 ($218,910 x 6% Rate of

Return) on the money he withdrew from the IRA. When both men were

alive, they each received Social Security benefits. Once Doctor Dan dies,

Baker Bob is able to collect Doctor Dan's higher benefit amount (assuming

they were married), but loses his own benefit of $15,616. The reduction in

his annual income of $28,751 ($13,135 investment income + $15,616 Social

Security) is enough to require Baker Bob to spend more of his IRA that he

inherited from Doctor Dan in order to support his lifestyle. This causes the

Married and Dies graph to continue a gradual decline at the levels illustrated.

In the Married and Lives graph, the investment income earned on Doctor

Dan's IRAs, combined with both men's Social Security Benefits, is more than enough to cover their annual living expenses: ($60,000 Annual investment income + $41,226 Doctor Dan's Social Security + $13,134 Baker Bob's Social Security = Annual Income of $114,360, less Annual Living Expenses of $75,000 = $39,360). This $39,360 surplus can be added to their savings every year, increasing the couple's total wealth. This also allows all of their combined savings to continue to grow beyond the remainder of their lives. (Sorry, that's a lot of details, but it's what we pride ourselves on doing.)

Now let's look at Baker Bob's inheritance, assuming that the couple ignored all of my advice and did *not* get married prior to Doctor Dan's death. Carried forward from our previous unmarried partners, Baker Bob's $50,000 savings account has now grown to $107,748. This is his own money, so there are no tax implications on the account when Doctor Dan dies. As an unmarried man, Doctor Dan had a traditional IRA with a balance of $857,750 when he passed away. Baker Bob must pay Pennsylvania inheritance tax on that entire amount. The 15% tax, or $128,663, totally wipes out his personal savings account balance. So again we start our graph with the tax adjusted *Inherited IRA* balance of $617,580 ($857,750 less 28% Federal Income Tax to give us the purchasing power of the IRA), and add Bob's own money of $107,748—

for a total $725,328. And once again, we see a significant decrease in assets

the very first year of our analysis. This decrease is caused by the large state

inheritance tax payment due the first year after Doctor Dan's death.

Even after the first year, we continue to see a rather steep reduction in assets

every year thereafter. Another downside to not getting married is that Baker

Bob can only collect the $5,000 (plus COLAs) in Social Security benefits

that he had been receiving since turning 62. This is not nearly enough to

cover his cost of living of $75,000 annually (plus COLAs). Not only must he

withdraw money from his *Inherited IRA* to cover living expenses, he must

also withdraw enough money to cover the income tax payments due on these

withdrawals. Because of Baker Bob's shortage of assets, his distributions

must be larger than the RMD under the "Not Married, Current Law"

scenario. This causes him to run out of assets within seven years of Doctor

Dan's death, preventing him from taking full advantage of the *stretch IRA*

(and more importantly, from eating).

Now let's look at what will happen to the unmarried survivor, if the law is

changed as we expect it to be. Baker Bob must take enough in distributions

to fully deplete the *Inherited IRA* within five years. We recommended that he

spread out these distributions as evenly as possible, in an effort to minimize the impact of the income tax due on the distributions. Unfortunately, Baker

Bob runs out of assets during the seventh year after Doctor Dan's death.

There is not a significant difference in asset growth/depletion between the

two unmarried scenarios, because in the example under the current law, Bob

spent more than the RMD and depleted the IRA in 7 years--similar spending

to this 5 year example. However, we chose to include both unmarried

options in our graph just to maintain consistency. In both unmarried

scenarios, Baker Bob runs out of money at the age of 86.

The assumptions for this graph include the following at the time of Doctor

Dan's death:

a.   Baker Bob held a few part time jobs over the years, but is

    unemployed at the age of 60

b.   Baker Bob has $107,748 of his own savings in after-tax assets

c.   If married, and using our strategies, Baker Bob inherits a traditional

    IRA from Doctor Dan worth $535,997 and a Roth IRA worth

    $603,405 (before tax implications)

d.   If unmarried, and not using our strategies, Baker Bob inherits a

    traditional IRA worth $857,750 (before tax implications)

e. For each scenario, assets are decreased in the first year for Pennsylvania inheritance tax under current law, which apply even to same-sex married couples. (I hope that changes by the time you read this, or at least in the next couple of years.)

f. Baker Bob elects to collect Social Security of $5,000 (plus COLAs) at age 62 if unmarried in the less favorable scenario, or $15,616 (plus COLAs) as a spousal benefit at age 66 if he and Doctor Dan were married and he's able to collect on Doctor Dan's earnings history.

g. During his life time, Doctor Dan Applied and Suspended his Social Security Benefits at age 66.

h. Annual living expenses, $75,000 (plus COLAs for inflation)

i. Includes 3% Rate of Inflation

j. Includes 6% Rate of Return

k. Balances shown include a 28% Federal Tax Allowance on traditional Retirement Account Balances.

l. We are measuring IRAs net of taxes. That means we are valuing a $1,000,000 IRA at $720,000 which is calculated by multiplying the IRA value times 28% tax rate (or $280,000), and subtracting the tax from the value of the account. This gives us the purchasing power of the IRA and allows us to add it to the after tax investments and the

Roth IRA for a net total.

So once again, we see the significance of the couple marrying. If the couple

marries, Doctor Dan can be assured that there will be enough spendable

assets to cover Baker Bob's expenses through the end of his life. If the

couple doesn't marry, given these assumptions, Baker Bob will run out of

money at the age of 86. Let's break down these differences. The *very first*

day that Baker Bob inherits the assets of husband Doctor Dan, he will have

$300,000 more, simply because the couple married. In addition, out of the

total inheritance from his spouse, Baker Bob would have received $603,405

in a Roth IRA. Baker Bob should spend any funds from the Traditional IRA

first, which allows the Roth IRA to continue to grow income tax free. Keep

in mind that, when the time comes that Baker Bob needs to withdraw funds

from the Roth IRA, all distributions, including the growth on the account,

will be 100% income tax free.

The first year after Doctor Dan's death would be the only year in which

married Baker Bob must withdraw more funds from his inheritance than he

would have to if he were unmarried. First, because he inherited $300,000

more as a married man, he must also pay more Pennsylvania inheritance tax.

If he were married, his total inheritance tax bill would be $170,910

($1,139,402 x 15%). If he were unmarried, his Pennsylvania inheritance tax

bill would be $128,663 ($857,750 x 15%). Not only would his inheritance

tax be less as an unmarried person, keep in mind that he also has $107,748 in

his own after tax savings account to cover a large portion of the tax bill. His

total IRA distributions during the first year after Doctor Dan's death would

have to be $204,684 ($75,000 Living Expenses + $170,910 Inheritance Tax -

$41,226 Social Security Income) if he were married, but only $90,915

($75,000 Living Expenses + $20,915 Inheritance Tax - $5,000 Social

Security Income) if he were unmarried. But even after paying more in taxes,

married Baker Bob still has a larger pile of money than unmarried Baker

Bob.

The second year after Doctor Dan's death, Baker Bob would be required to

pay federal income taxes on the large distributions that he took the first year.

If he was married, the income taxes for year two would be approximately

$48,000, and if unmarried, $20,000. As a result, year two's distributions

would be $81,774 if married ($75,000 Living Expenses + $48,000 Income

Tax - $41,226 Social Security Income), and if unmarried, $90,000 ($75,000

Living Expenses + $20,000 Income Tax - $5,000 Social Security Income).

Once the tax implications of the original distributions have been paid, Baker

Bob's annual distributions become more reasonable. If Baker Bob were married, he would only need to take distributions of $33,774 plus income taxes due, for the remainder of his life ($75,000 living expenses - $41,226 in Social Security Income). This means that his rolled over traditional IRA would be depleted within five years, and he would only owe tax on an additional three years of distributions. After the traditional IRA is depleted in year five, he would have to begin withdrawing funds from his inherited Roth IRA. The distributions from the Roth IRA are 100% income tax free to Baker Bob.

If Baker Bob remained unmarried, his distributions from the traditional IRA would need to be much larger. This is because, as an unmarried person, Baker Bob would be receiving only $5,000 per year in Social Security benefits and all other money necessary for his financial survival would come from his inheritance. So, not only does he have to take larger distributions, but all those distributions are coming from an *Inherited IRA*—which means that the distributions are 100% taxable. His annual distributions would need to be around $85,000 a year ($75,000 living expenses + $15,000 income taxes - $5,000 Social Security Income). At this rate in either unmarried scenario, Baker Bob would run out of all assets before his eighty-sixth birthday.

We assume that Baker Bob will live to the age of 90. Think of the stress that he and Penniless Perry will endure trying to finance those last four years, since Baker Bob and Doctor Dan never married. If they had married, Baker Bob would never have had to worry about being a burden to his son. And what a wonderful legacy the couple could leave to Baker Bob's son—a tax free Roth IRA worth $578,548.

The Case Study Continues With the Second Death—What About the Next Generation?

It is clear that, if Baker Bob and Doctor Dan plan according to our strategies, there will be assets remaining even after Baker Bob has died. So if we now bring Penniless Perry into the picture, we can see how the differences between using our strategies and maintaining the status quo will affect the next generation.

Let's Take a Look at the Long Term Growth Potential for the Couple's Heir if They Follow All of the Advice in This Book

Penniless Perry is the underemployed adopted son of Baker Bob. He worked as an untenured faculty member doing research at the age of 50 when his father, Bob, passed away just before his ninety-first birthday. Although he earned about $60,000 per year, Penniless routinely spent almost every penny that he earned. Saving and preparing for retirement was never a high priority. He never thought about what would happen to him if he retired or lost his income. Prior to his father passing away, Penniless Perry's entire savings consisted of $10,500 in a local bank account.

If you recall from the previous graph, in both of the examples where Baker Bob and Doctor Dan did not marry, there are no assets left for Penniless Perry to inherit by the time Baker Bob dies. Penniless will have to continue to work the rest of his life to support his $1,000/week lifestyle, since his Social Security income will be insufficient. And who knows what will happen if he is unable to work in his later years?

But married Doctor Dan and Baker Bob were thinking ahead to safeguard Penniless Perry's financial security. When Baker Bob died, he left the balance of the assets that he had inherited from Doctor Dan, to Penniless Perry. After taxes, Perry was the proud owner of an *Inherited Roth IRA* worth $578,548. Penniless Perry thought it was criminal that he had to spend more than his life savings to pay Pennsylvania inheritance tax of 4.5% (note: children get a break on inheritance tax in Pennsylvania), which amounted to $26,035.

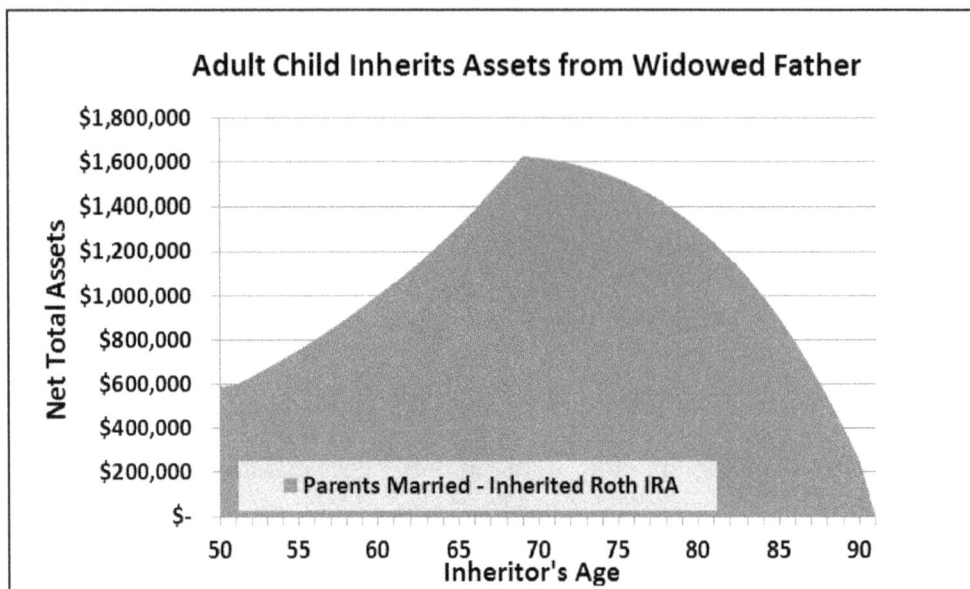

Adult Child Inherits Assets from Widowed Father

The assumptions for this graph include the following:

a. Penniless Perry is employed and earns $60,000 annually through age 69 (plus COLAs)

b. Penniless Perry retires at age 70 collecting Social Security Benefits of $20,000 (plus COLAs)

c. Penniless Perry at the age of 60 inherits a Roth IRA from his widowed father, $578,548

d. Annual living expenses, $52,000 (plus COLAs)

e. Includes 3% Rate of Inflation

f. Includes 6% Rate of Return.

The inheritance and the process of dealing with his father's death was a wakeup call for Penniless Perry. After getting some reasonable retirement planning advice, he learned that if he continues to responsibly invest the Roth IRA in a well-diversified set of index funds, he may be able to retire securely if he continues to work through the age of 69. At age 70 he can retire and stop working completely, and then be able to collect $20,000 (plus COLAs) in Social Security benefits from age 70 forward. Let's take a look at the graph of Penniless Perry's inheritance. In the illustration above, we see the addition of his father's Roth IRA of about $590,000. Notice how his earnings remain stagnant the first year. This is consistent with prior scenarios, where the state inheritance tax is due the year following an inheritance. In the state of Pennsylvania, the Inheritance Tax Rate for a child of the decedent is 4½%. After the first year, Penniless's inherited assets continue to grow until he retires at age 70. Although he is required to take distributions from his *Inherited Roth IRA*, he invests the proceeds in an after-tax account and grows that for his retirement years as well.

Once he retires, his annual living expenses exceed his Social Security income, resulting in a rapid decline of his savings. Keep in mind that the only reason this inheritance exists is because Doctor Dan and Baker Bob took my retirement and estate planning advice. Otherwise, there would have been nothing for Penniless Perry to inherit. By the time Penniless Perry

retires at age 70, his savings have grown by over a million dollars. This gives

him enough funds so that he can retire and live the lifestyle to which he has

become accustomed through the age of 90. If his parents had not taken my

advice, Penniless Perry truly would be penniless.

Are you considering navigating these potentially rocky waters without a
professional who is qualified and experienced in distribution and estate
planning for IRAs and retirement plans? Are you prepared to consider the
interplay of the various strategic options for Social Security, Roth
conversions, and retirement plan distributions? Are you clear about how
marriage would affect your finances?

Please be sure to work with a trusted advisor, who can "run the numbers"
for your unique situation and help you to make the ideal choices for your
retirement plan, social security, Roth conversions, wills, and trusts. Avoid
the pitfalls by choosing the right professional.

Final Note

I have included the level of detail and quantitative explanation in this final

chapter and throughout the book because I don't take advice like "I think you

should marry your partner for financial purposes" lightly. I want you to

know all the financial advantages and disadvantages of getting married

before you make a decision to marry or stay single. I also want you to take

the appropriate actions after you get married or if you are already married.

I hope I have proven to you, that subject to limited exceptions, most same-sex couples when at least one partner is 60 or older would be significantly financially better off if they got married. You would also be better off taking some of the pro-active steps outlined in the book after you get married.

Yes, hopefully you received great information packaged the best way I know how. What I haven't stressed is the improved quality of life for you and your partner and eventual heirs that you can achieve—but only if you take action. I really want you to act on what you have read. If you are in a long-term committed relationship, either on your own or preferably with the help of the appropriate advisor or advisors, make a plan and then implement the steps to achieve your plan. If you do, drop me a line. I would love to hear from you.

Appendix: How We "Run the Numbers"

To create the charts and the numbers referenced in *Retire Secure! for Same Sex Couples,* we had to "run the numbers"— and, literally, we've spent hundreds of hours refining our calculations. We have not only run the numbers for our original Roth IRA conversion article, but also for two our best-selling editions of *Retire Secure!* (Wiley, 2006 and 2009) and *The Roth Revolution, Pay Taxes Once and Never Again.* (Morgan James, 2011).

Running the numbers can mean different things to different people, so I will give a brief description of what we mean, and how we ran the numbers for *Retire Secure! for Same Sex Couples.* This explanation will emphasize the Roth IRA conversion component of running the numbers because we don't cover that topic in great detail in this book.

In the old days, before the existence of some of the wonderful specialized software that we have today, running the numbers meant testing different scenarios with an Excel spreadsheet and 1040 preparation software. My wife, Cindy Lange (a software engineer), and I developed a basic model using Excel that was really an unpublished Excel template. We would input different variables and construct complex formulas to help us project a long-term financial outcome for a married couple, given certain assumptions and different courses of action. Currently, that might seem bit primitive, but we still have clients—engineers and quantitative types—who come to us with their own numbers generated through this type of calculation. Later, Steve Kohman, CPA, who is the senior "number runner" in our office, took that primitive template and made significant improvements. We called it *Money for Life*.

We used Steve's *Money for Life* program to run the numbers for our 1998 Roth IRA article, which was peer-reviewed and published by the American Institute of CPAs. They insisted we send in all our formulas, calculations and spreadsheets. The methodology and results were scrutinized closely by a team of CPA's, and had to pass muster before the article could even be published. But that was our start. It was cutting edge analysis at the time, and, even though specialized software is available today, we believe the key to "running the numbers" is having a core understanding of the issues and being able to test different fact patterns to arrive at the best conclusion. For the calculations used in the book today, we stayed true to our roots. We have, however, incorporated specialized software programs for IRAs and Roth IRA conversions, Social Security calculations, minimum required distribution calculations, and sophisticated income tax software. Personalized projections based on those calculations are what we provide for our clients when we analyze the "suitability" of Roth IRA conversions as a component of their big picture planning.   For the purposes of *Retire Secure! for Same Sex Couples*, we optimized the amount and timing of Roth IRA conversions in the "married, take Social Security and do Roth IRA conversions" scenario.

Steve Kohman, CPA and Shirl Trefelner, CPA, both full-time employees at our office, did all the calculations for *Retire Secure! for Same Sex Couples* and I owe them a debt of gratitude—they did many of these calculations right in the middle of tax season, which for them is the busiest time of the year! Running the numbers for Roth IRA conversions is different than you might expect. Even today with all the wonderful software, you can't just plop in some numbers and click "Maximize." You have to think about alternatives and options, and try multiple combinations and variables. Let me give you an idea of the complexity of this question. One calculation might ignore Roth IRA conversions completely. The other extreme assumes that the taxpayer converts the entire IRA to a Roth IRA, in one tax year. Another scenario might have the taxpayer converting an amount that would create taxable income that would be taxed at the top of the 15% bracket every year between his/her retirement and the year that he/she has to start taking required minimum distributions from the IRA. Or, suppose the taxpayer had a compelling reason to convert at a quicker rate that resulted in him/her being taxed at the top of the 25% bracket every year. A variation on that might be to convert to the top of the 25% bracket for two years and then, closer to age 70, convert to the top of the 15% bracket, etc. The possibilities are endless, and it's important to know that an action that works well for another couple might be financially devastating for you.

Rather than make assumptions, we have to test our results using 1040 software to avoid any surprises. The increased income from a conversion can actually reduce the alternative minimum tax, but increase or cause the phase out of itemized deductions, increased capital gains rate or taxation of qualified dividends, increased taxes due to Social Security benefits received, or even an increase in the Medicare Part B premium. I can't understand how someone can legitimately claim to "run the numbers" unless they test their results with 1040 software. Some of the 1040 checking is so tricky that I would not feel comfortable with anyone but a CPA with a lot of income-tax preparation experience testing the results that we get from the specialized software and Excel spreadsheets.

We are not fans of the Roth IRA calculators that do-it-yourselfers can find on the internet. My fear with some of those calculators is that they are used by people who don't understand the complexities of Roth IRA conversions

or other relevant tax laws, and a simplified analysis might accidentally lead

to a terrible outcome.

Married vs. Unmarried
Net Assets Available for Retirement Years

(Chart: Net Assets vs. Age)

- **Married, SS Apply & Suspend, Roth Conversions**
- **Unmarried, SS at 62, No Roth Conversions**

Vertical axis (Net Assets): $-, $500,000, $1,000,000, $1,500,000, $2,000,000, $2,500,000

Horizontal axis (Age): 62, 67, 72, 77, 82, 87, 92, 97

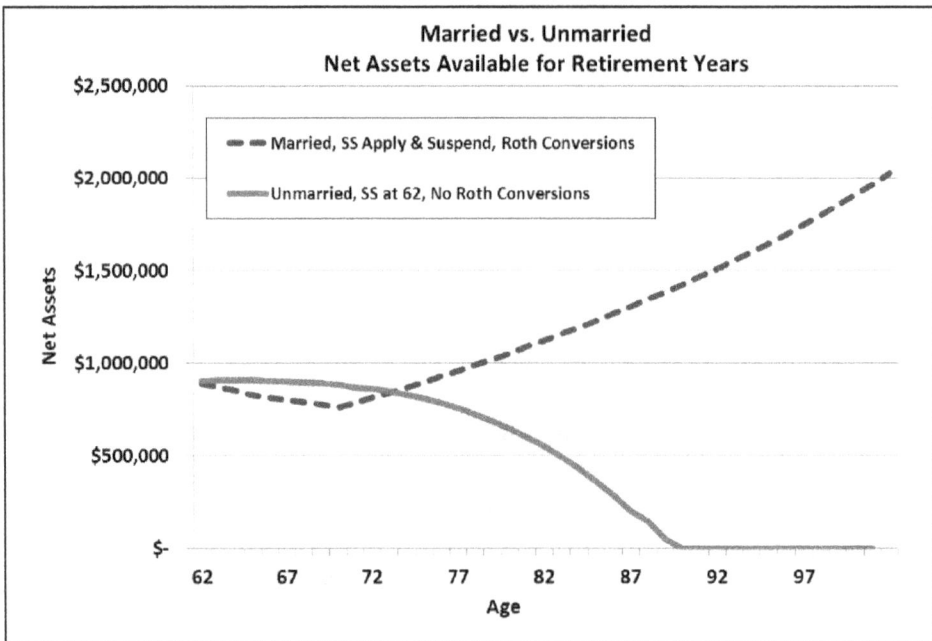

We also have software that tests the outcomes when different Social Security

strategies are used. Then we found that the Social Security calculations and

the Roth IRA conversion calculations are not independent, but interrelated

and work synergistically. We haven't yet figured out a formula or algorithm

for that, so we use some rules-of-thumb and our judgment to decide what

numbers to test. We also have to consider how long the money will be

invested, and what rates of return will be earned. Frankly, the way we run the numbers is both an art and a science.

The following graph, which we include in our introduction and in our "Putting it All Together" (Chapter 8), was one of the toughest to run the numbers for. (In this example, we ignore one partner dying before the other partner and we ignore the next generation, but in Chapter 8, we include the analysis where one partner dies, the surviving partner inherits, and eventually that partner dies leaving what is left to the next generation.)

To arrive at these results, we tested a lot of scenarios using multiple Roth IRA conversion strategies, and different timings for taking Social Security benefits. Holding off on applying for Social Security until age 66, then using the Apply and Suspend strategy, and doing a series of Roth IRA conversions starting at age 62 worked out the best for our married couple who was pro-active with their planning. It also passes the "does that seem right" test, because holding off on Social Security left the same-sex married couple in a low tax bracket—which made Roth IRA conversions that much more favorable. The growth trend recovers (the dotted blue line) when the couple begins collecting significantly increased Social Security at 70. So, staying single, taking Social Security early, and not making any Roth IRA conversions (the solid red line), while favorable for a little over 10 years, becomes much worse in the long run.

For our graph, we chose a couple with $700,000 in a traditional IRA, $400,000 in after tax assets, and annual expenses of $75,000. For smaller estates, the differences would likely be less, but perhaps saving $200,000 on a $500,000 estate is worth more in human terms than saving $500,000 on a $1,000,000 estate. For larger estates, the difference could be enormous— especially if you consider the benefit to the next generation (or even next two generations).

I will concede that we did not use random numbers to determine how much money the couple had at the age of 62. We picked scenarios that I thought would be close to what many of our readers actually have in their investments. We also picked scenarios where the difference between using our strategies and doing nothing was the most significant. I like looking at the chart and saying "If you use my strategies, you will have $1,500,000 and if you don't, you will be broke." But, while this particular chart shows a huge advantage, for almost all the numbers we looked at, there were still significant financial benefits to our approach.

If we had had the luxury of time, it would have been wonderful to have this chart peer reviewed before I published it. Frankly, the last time we went through that process, there was close to a year's lag between when I submitted the first draft and the final publication of the article. (By the way, in 1998, our Roth IRA conversion article tied for *The Tax Adviser's* "best article of the year.") I believe this information is too important—right now—for the LGBT community to wait for the peer review process.

purposes only and does not constitute legal or professional tax advice or the

advertisement of legal services. Readers must rely on the advice of their

own tax and legal counsel. The advice and strategies contained herein may

not be suitable for every situation as consequences vary depending upon

individual circumstances. If professional assistance is required, the services

of a competent professional person should be sought. The Author shall not

be liable for any loss of profit or any other commercial damages, including

but not limited to special, incidental, consequential, or other damages. The

fact that an organization or website is referred to in this work as a citation

and/or a potential source of further information does not mean that the

Author endorses the information the organization or website may provide or

recommendations it may make. Furthermore, readers should be aware that

internet websites listed in this work may have changed or disappeared

between when this work was written and when it is read.

About the Author
James Lange, CPA/Attorney

Attorney/CPA James Lange started the first estate planning website for same-sex couples, www.outestateplanning.com, in Pittsburgh in 2002. With 30 years of retirement and estate planning experience, Lange and his team have drafted more than 1,800 wills and trusts. Jim is the author of two bestselling books including *Retire Secure! Pay Taxes Later* (Wiley, 2006 and 2009), which was endorsed by Charles Schwab, Larry King, Ed Slott, Jane Bryant Quinn, Roger Ibbotson, and Burton Malkiel and dozens of other financial experts. Jim also wrote *The Roth Revolution, Pay Taxes Once and Never Again* (Morgan James, 2011), which was endorsed by Ed Slott, Natalie Choate and Bob Keebler and many others. He is the creator of **Lange's Cascading Beneficiary Plan™** and **The Roth IRA Institute**.

Jim's strategies have been endorsed by *The New York Times*, *The Wall Street Journal* (30 times), *Newsweek*, *Money Magazine*, *Smart Money*, *Reader's Digest*, *Financial Planning*, *Bottom Line*, *Kiplinger's*, and many other publications. His articles have appeared in *Bottom Line*, *Financial Planning*, *The Tax Adviser* (the peer reviewed journal of the AICPA), and the *Journal of Retirement Planning*. Most recently, *PA Lawyer Magazine* published in their January/February 2014 issue, Jim's article, "The Demise of Federal DOMA, New Financial Planning Strategies for Same-Sex Couples."

Audio archives and most transcripts of 110 hours of Jim's radio show, *The Lange Money Hour*, are available at www.paytaxeslater.com.